YOU and the INTERNET of THINGS

A practical guide to understanding and integrating the IoT into your daily life

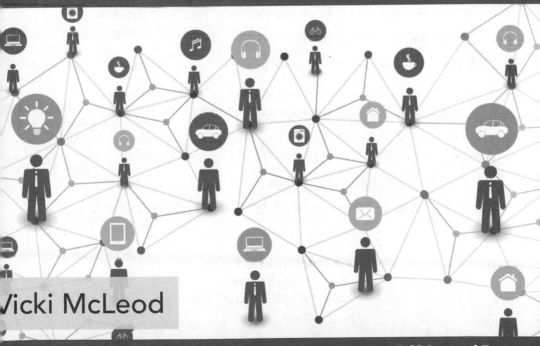

Vicki McLeod

Self-Counsel Press
(a division of)
International Self-Counsel Press Ltd.
Canada   USA

Self-Counsel Press acknowledges the financial support of the Government of Canada through the Canada Book Fund (CBF) for our publishing activities. Canadä

Printed in Canada.

First edition: 2020

Library and Archives Canada Cataloguing in Publication

Title: You and the internet of things : a practical guide to understanding and integrating the IoT into your daily life / Vicki McLeod.

Names: McLeod, Vicki, author.

Series: Self-Counsel reference series.

Description: 1st edition. | Series statement: Reference series

Identifiers: Canadiana (print) 2020017388X | Canadiana (ebook) 20200173928 | ISBN 9781770403239 (softcover) | ISBN 9781770405080 (EPUB) | ISBN 9781770405097 (Kindle)

Subjects: LCSH: Internet of things.

Classification: LCC TK5105.8857 .M35 2020 | DDC 004.67/8—dc23

Self-Counsel Press
(a division of)
International Self-Counsel Press Ltd.

North Vancouver, BC Canada	Bellingham, WA USA

Contents

Notice to Readers

Laws and technology are constantly changing. Every effort is made to keep this publication as current as possible. However, the author, the publisher, and the vendor of this book make no representations or warranties regarding the outcome or the use to which the information in this book is put and are not assuming any liability for any claims, losses, or damages arising out of the use of this book. The reader should not rely on the author or the publisher of this book for any professional advice. Please be sure that you have the most recent edition.

To my mother, Beda Martin, for her endless curiosity and open-mindedness. The world desperately needs both and I am grateful to have inherited my share from her.

Acknowledgments

For Ian, who is everything, most especially an urban planning nerd and excellent researcher. Thank you for your contributions to our beautiful life and to these pages.

Much gratitude goes to my amazing editor Eileen Velthuis for her fine eye and sure hand in shaping this book. A number of professional resources made this book possible. It simply could not have been written without the technology insight, wisdom, expertise, and patient good humor of my long-time friend and colleague, Steve Dotto of DottoTech.com. Don Lekei, founder and owner of Help My Tech has been a reliable go-to resource for technology troubleshooting and expertise both personally and professionally. I thank him for his willing input here, and also for reminding me of Arthur C. Clarke's Third Law.

I am also grateful for the good-natured answering of many questions and the insights offered by more recent acquaintances: John Biehler, tech journalist and editorial director of GetConnected Media, and Rob Richardson, Senior National Account Manager for Arlo Technologies in Canada. Thank you, too, to Ryan Bradt, Sean Crocker, Dr. Kendall Ho, Mark Milner, and Ginger Purgatoria for personal interviews. I would also like to make mention of the work of US-based

Stacey Higginbotham. *Stacey on IoT* is a news publication covering the Internet of Things. Her website, podcast, blogs, and articles were an invaluable resource to me. A special shout-out to Clayton Brown and Allen LaRose and the many technology experts and enthusiasts online and offline whose free and generous sharing of information and knowledge is helping us all learn to live with and understand the sometimes daunting world of technology.

I am very grateful for the contributions and support of my peers, friends, family, and colleagues. They shared their personal experiences as well as tea, texts, and much loving encouragement: Bosco Anthony, Fred Armstrong, Kallan Armstrong, Rebecca Coleman, Angela Crocker, Valerie Dingwall, Marian Dodds, Debra Dunsmore, Kim Louise Easterbrook, Kimmy Finnsson, Nathan Hyam, Paul Holmes, Faye Luxemburg-Hyam, Cadi Jordan, Seija Juoksu, Joseph Kakwinokanasum, Hadis Kiani, Dominic Kotarski, C.K. Lee, Sean Moffitt, Etanda Morelli, Russell McKewan, Farid Poursoltani, Shelley Schroeder, Sylvia Taylor, Michael Trawick, Rebecca Vaughn, Christina Waschko, Linette Weibe, Ann Wilson, and those who prefer to remain anonymous.

This book was written on the unceded territory of the Snuneymuxw First Nation, a Coast Salish people. Their beautiful land is located in the center of Coast Salish territory on the eastern coast of Vancouver Island in British Columbia, Canada. I thank them for the privilege of living and working here.

Preface

Any sufficiently advanced technology is indistinguishable from magic.

— ARTHUR C. CLARKE
Profiles of the Future (revised edition, 1973)

In 2018, I applied to enter Simon Fraser University's The Writer's Studio Program. SFU is well-respected Canadian university and the program is highly regarded among writers. The Studio is offered either in person at the university's downtown campus or as a distance learning option. At the time, I lived in a Vancouver suburb that is an hour's drive from the downtown campus. I selected and was accepted by the campus-based program. One of the key reasons I chose to commute to classes rather than enjoy the convenience of the online program was that I wanted to be part of a community of writers, and as a baby boomer, I tend toward a preference for face-to-face engagement.

Once enrolled, my peers and I shared a desire to discuss our ongoing work outside of the formal Studio setting. However, we were hampered not only by the geographic distance between us but also by the unevenness of our individual adaptation to using communication technologies. The program itself was wonderful and I have no hesitation recommending it, but while commonly used cloud-based video conferencing tools such as Zoom, and software platforms such as Skype could have enabled us to communicate in real-time via video in between formal classes, there was an uneven distribution of computer skills and tech savvy amongst participants. This created a barrier to participation outside of face-to-face or in-class sessions.

This is one of the major challenges with technology. Not all users are created equal, and not all technology is simple to access. In the words of William Gibson, the American-Canadian speculative fiction writer, "The future is already here. It's just not evenly distributed yet." (*The Economist*, Dec. 4, 2003)

In part, I wrote this book to address a gap I see in the average consumer's understanding of the impact of the internet and the possibilities and potential afforded by a networked environment on our daily lives. If you are a techno-geek, a coder, or an early adapter to new technologies, this book isn't for you. You will already have an advanced understanding of the IoT and a deep personal or professional interest in the evolution of digital technology, and feel comfortable about making intelligent choices that impact your home, health, transportation, and leisure options. You will also have a good grasp of the cost of such technologies, the learning curve required to integrate them into daily life, and an awareness of the prevalent privacy and security concerns.

If, however, like me, you lived a good portion of your life in a wholly analog environment, you know the mental shift required to embrace the internet and the digital age. If you were born before about 1985, you didn't grow up with the internet, and you are not a digital native. Instead, you are what my good friend and colleague Steve Dotto, founder of DottoTech who is known as Canada's favorite geek, calls a digital refugee. You are new(ish) to learning the culture, language, and etiquettes of a brave new online world. And, like actual refugees, in some ways we are being forced to learn and adapt. We need supportive translators and guides, helping us find a way to navigate unfamiliar territory.

I was also inspired to write this book by my mother. In 2018, Angela Crocker and I coauthored *Digital Legacy Plan: A Guide to the Personal and Practical Elements of Your Digital Life Before You Die*

(Self-Counsel Press 2019). My mom, an avid reader with a deeply curious mind, read the book cover-to-cover in just a couple of days. I had hand-delivered her copy and during our visit, when she was already deep into the book, my very intelligent 80-year old Mom peeked over the cover and said, "Honey, what's a URL?"

Let me be clear. While my mother is not internet-savvy, she has and uses a smartphone, and she and her life partner use his personal computer for email to keep in touch with friends and family and to research, plan, and book travel and entertainment. They enjoy watching their Smart TV and using the Global Positioning System in their SUV. Neither of them can be characterized as "dear old things" wandering off into their sunset years. Mom recently celebrated her 80th birthday with a 40-day South Pacific cruise and plans to continue to travel the world and live a fully engaged life. However, she struggles to keep up with the terminology and the rapidly changing technological world. Because she is lively, vital, and endlessly curious she has a keen sense of the fear of missing out, what the kids call FOMO. She wants to know what's currently trending on Twitter, and to discuss what's popular on Netflix. She wants access to the gadgets and systems that will simplify everyday activities, and to participate in digital health solutions that will aid her quest for healthy longevity. More than that she wants a basic understanding of the risks and benefits of a networked digital life, and to be able to make intelligent choices about what to invest in.

This book isn't exclusively for the scenario of the 80-year-old parent I've outlined here, but if you are dealing with aging parents and have become the de facto tech support and family IT person, this book will help you help them. More importantly, if you, like me, are straddling the digital and analog worlds, or are part of the sandwich generation, assisting aging parents or relatives, while supporting young adults who may need to make a significant investment in changing technology — and navigating these advances in your own life, this book can help you as well.

I am the right guide for this journey. In the early '90s, I started encouraging clients to consider creating websites to get their message out and connect with customers and stakeholders. The internet was new, and the governments, not-for-profit agencies, and businesses I worked with then were cautious about this new technology. Nearly 20 years later I found myself making the same arguments to clients about establishing social media profiles, working with hundreds of businesses, organizations, and individuals to help them overcome their reluctance to engage in social networking and the normal fear of investing in the unknown. In addition to nearly a decade of writing newspaper columns about the intersection of the analog and digital worlds, this is my third book related to digital topics. I predict that the IoT is the next big technological advancement that mainstream consumers need to deal with.

And, much as I did in the early days of websites and social media, I hope to provide some practical insight and useful tools to help you, dear reader, develop a level of comfort as you navigate myriad choices and opportunities.

Introduction

As a result of advances to sophisticated artificial intelligence, machine learning, automation, and augmented and virtual reality, the internet landscape is undergoing massive change. The internet is no longer just about accessing information via electronic devices such as laptops, smartphones, and tablets. From toasters to transit systems, we are now in the age of the Internet of Things (IoT) where interconnected devices and objects are fully networked and communicate data back and forth. Devices and objects learn from these data exchanges and adapt and respond to our personal needs and preferences.

From "smart" houses to "smart" cars, from cashless banking to wearable sensors that gather personal health data, new technological innovations and the resulting IoT are integrated with nearly all aspects of daily living, impacting health, home, transportation, shopping, travel, and entertainment. Soon, everything will be "smart."

What does this mean for you? This book is a guide to understanding the effects of soon-to-be common technologies on your daily life and how to use these technologies for increased safety, security, convenience, and quality of life. Whether you are a mainstream user of technology, part of the sandwich generation — that is, somewhere between caring for aging parents and still supporting children, or a baby boomer trying to navigate the IoT age, this book is your roadmap. If you are not familiar with internet terminology, explanations of common terms are provided throughout the book. Even if you are not a user of computers, you are no doubt a user of things, and as more and more of the objects and gadgets we interact with daily become computerized and linked to the internet, you too will be transformed into a smart technology user. It is already becoming difficult to buy common consumer products such as a television set or a refrigerator that are "dumb" or not somehow connected to something else.

1. What Is the Internet of Things?

In simplest terms, the Internet of Things can be defined as the interconnection via the internet of computing devices embedded in everyday objects, enabling them to send and receive data without requiring human-to-human or human-to-computer interaction. This interconnection and data collection and analysis is what makes our homes, cars, and coffeepots "smart." In other words, our devices, appliances, vehicles, and houses are beginning to think for themselves.

Our smartphones have connected us to everything, and have become the hub, or central brain, that controls and integrates various apps, devices, and objects that can make up a user's personal IoT network. The smartphone is at the heart of the conversation among the "things," and typical smartphone use has moved far beyond its original purpose as a mobile telephone. In this book, we'll discuss the importance of the smartphone as a hub and look at other kinds of hubs. What are the key devices, apps, and functions needed to support the personal IoT network? How do these integrate with laptops, tablets, and intelligent virtual voice assistants such as Amazon's Alexa, Google's Google Assistant, and Apple's Siri? What are these assistants, how do they work, and what are the risks?

There are widespread concerns about the Internet of Things in regard to data collection and privacy, as well as justifiable fears about the overall security of integrated internet systems. We live in a time when we are trading privacy for convenience. I will aim to offer some reassurances and resources and look at what you can (and can't) do to safeguard privacy.

There is still some distance to go in terms of efficient and affordable fully networked systems. Even though appliances and devices are equipped with the necessary microchips, sensors, and enabling technology, the tools and protocols are not yet standardized to enable devices with different vendor origins to communicate effectively. Smartphone apps, communication hubs, and cloud-based services are enabling us to control many elements of life remotely, but the sophisticated networks to run them are not yet fully synchronized. This is something we need to consider if our goal is a simple, affordable, and easy-to-manage system.

Systems are becoming more sophisticated all the time. I opened this book with a quote from Arthur C. Clarke: "Any sufficiently advanced technology is indistinguishable from magic." Of course, technology is not magic. It may seem so, simply because as laypeople we do not fully understand it. We find the terminology baffling and the scope and scale overwhelming. It may seem that IT people and technology experts are performing a kind of magic, having the special knowledge they do about what can seem to be a mysterious and mystifying world. Luckily, experts are available to us to help with specific problems and advice online and offline. As consumers, what we need to do is prepare to learn and to adapt as IoT technology changes. This book will help you do that.

2. How to Use This Book

This book offers a high-level look at the world of the Internet of Things as it relates to home life, leisure and entertainment options, health, and daily living. Together we'll explore how networked living offers a multitude of options in terms of lifestyle, convenience, cost savings, and the personalization of goods and services. It is by no means a definitive guide. The subject matter is simply too vast. My perspective is a practical one.

As a consultant and a coach, the big questions I always ask when embarking on a project or a set of new strategies are: What is needed here? What would be most useful? It would not be possible for a single book to capture the amazing array of technological choices available to us in today's world. Even as I write this sentence technology is advancing at lightning speed. This book also does not make a moral judgment about the current or future applications of artificial intelligence, robotics, or machine learning. There are many books and resources available on those subjects and many more that discuss the impact of the IoT on business and industry.

To answer my own question here, what is needed is a broad and basic understanding of the IoT and its terminology and acronyms such as virtual reality (VR), artificial intelligence (AI), and augmented reality (AR), to name a few. We need to understand and not fear machine learning and its impact on everyday life. What will be most useful is a set of tools to help make informed, cost-effective, and safe choices. Specific products, brands, and resources are mentioned throughout to provide examples and to help you sort through the many choices available. Their mention does not necessarily imply endorsement or recommendation. I encourage you to consult with product experts and do your own research. This book is not a technical guide to setting up or troubleshooting IoT systems, although I do offer tips and insights and some guidance to help inform your choices.

Smart products will come complete with instructions on installation, maintenance, and troubleshooting, and most will have online support available 24/7. As you make decisions about the role of the IoT in your daily life, remember our friends Google and YouTube, where you can search and find up-to-date, detailed how-to information on just about everything. Throughout this book I have included the advice and insight of a number of technology and IoT experts and where they can be found online. This book also includes a downloadable kit of worksheets (see the back of the book for a web link where you can find this) that you can personalize to help you navigate the world of the Internet of Things — our world — and make sensible choices. Hopefully, it will also help increase your awareness of the role and limitations of technology in your life and in the lives of your families.

While working on this manuscript, I joined a set of older family cousins for a holiday celebration. It was hosted by my aunt and uncle, both in their 70s. They are fit and active baby boomers who golf almost daily and travel extensively. My aunt, a self-proclaimed internet luddite, is happily using the IoT in the form of a Golf Buddy, a wearable GPS analysis tool to improve her golf game. My uncle is pondering the purchase of a fully robotic lawn mower. Our visiting cousins use FaceTime and Skype to stay connected with children and grandchildren while they travel, having mapped the driving route to us on their GPS. Technology touches on nearly all aspects of our lives. It is important that we use it wisely, trusting in our capacity to adapt to it and understand it.

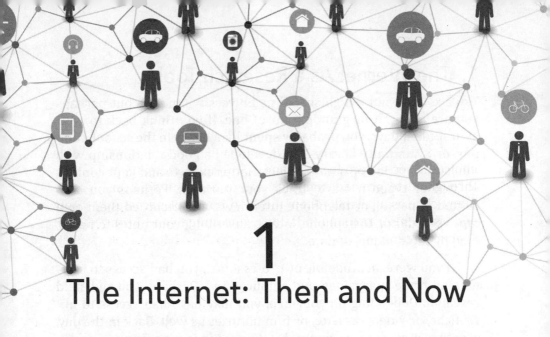

1
The Internet: Then and Now

As discussed in the introduction, we are in a new age where everything is connected to everything else. Before we get into detail about the revolutionary changes and adaptations enabled by the age of the IoT and how these might make your life easier, simpler, and more productive (or more fun!), let's spend some time examining where we currently find ourselves in terms of the digital world.

The early stages of the internet connected people to devices, data, and data management processes. Through personal computers we could connect not only to a staggering amount of information and data, but also to each other, first via message boards and email, and during the last decade, through initial social networking sites such as Facebook, Twitter, and LinkedIn.

Today, 40 percent of the world's population uses the internet. That is more than 3.9 billion people. More than 570 new websites are created every 60 seconds, and there are over 3.5 billion daily searches on Google. Per minute, 340,000 tweets are sent, with 500 million sent every day. Facebook has more than 2 billion active users with an average of 155 friends. Nearly 90 percent of the world's data has been created in the last two to three years. Most of us know and have used the internet as a tool for research, planning, and communication.

1. The Internet As a Research Tool

You are likely not a high school or university student, but perhaps you are a parent or grandparent of one. If you think back to your own student days, you probably spent long hours in the school, campus, or community library. You developed a good relationship with the local librarian or other subject matter experts and kept copious written or typed notes to track your research. Perhaps you conducted in-person or telephone interviews, and recorded them on a tape recorder or Dictaphone, later transcribing your notes to paper, filed by topic, name, or date.

If you were an academic or professional, you had access to journals or trade magazines and publications. Perhaps you did field research. Depending on your age, you may have had access to microfiche, or video, cassette, or film libraries as well. Back in the day, access to research was external — housed in institutions and somewhat difficult to access.

Even if you weren't a student, teacher, or industry professional, but simply a layperson with a practical need — say, for example you were planning a trip, or looking for a specific kind of professional or useful assistance — you needed either a referral from a trustworthy source, or you went to an expert, such as a travel agent, for example. Remember the Yellow Pages, the thick printed directory of businesses organized by category?

The internet changed all that. Essentially, the world wide web put the world of information at our fingertips. Via personal computers, we now have a single source for information. In reality, nearly everyone can get any information they need from a single desktop computer, laptop, tablet, or smartphone. You can easily store and archive anything that you need or that captures your interest, whether for personal, educational, or professional use. Digital information is here to stay, not subject to the degradation process that affects print and various kinds of film and tape. While the technology itself may change (remember floppy disks?), most hardware and software providers offer regular upgrades and updates to keep present-day technology current. The kind of information we have access to has also changed dramatically. Unlike traditional books, journals, or recordings, we can now access real-time audio, video, and live streaming on nearly any subject. This is "just-in-time" knowledge.

In terms of the internet as a research tool, it is not without concerns. Information on the internet changes and multiplies at a dizzying pace. The upside is that information can be constantly updated to maintain currency, and staying up to date is simplified for the researcher. The downside is that these resources are ephemeral. Websites may be neglected, and valuable information can be lost or ignored. Systems that are owned by government, nonprofits, businesses, schools, or individuals require human or financial resources and these may not be sustained over time. As well, a typical web search will return thousands of hits. Search algorithms have become extremely sophisticated (we'll deal more with this later) but it is still incumbent on the user to filter through the sites to weed out those that may be useless.

There is also an ongoing concern about the veracity or authority of online sources. Most professional or trade journals have a vetting process that includes meeting certain editorial standards for publication. Libraries and institutions have selection criteria for the purchasing of resources. The internet does not have these safeguards in place. In a way, the internet is a kind of wild west, enabling anyone with an opinion and basic technology skills the opportunity to present themselves as a subject matter expert via personal websites, blogs, or engagement in online forums and chat threads. In terms of online research, it is user beware. Users must exercise diligence and healthy skepticism in selecting online references and sources.

As I write this on my trusty laptop, I am referencing the work of other authors that I have downloaded onto my Kindle app on my tablet. My smartphone is by my side for quick Google searches. Several website tabs are open, and I am clipping references and resources to Evernote, appropriately tagged and notated. As a professional writer, the internet and its tools have made my job vastly easier. While early microprocessors purchased for home use were largely employed as video game consoles, rapid advances in technology and its applications, followed by the emergence of the Internet — the global system of interconnected networks and protocols that linked devices worldwide — enabled almost instant real-time communication. This convergence gave birth to new services such as email, internet telephony, internet television, online music, digital newspapers, and video streaming websites.

2. The Internet As a Communication Tool

For much of the last two decades our linked devices have provided us with an unparalleled ability to communicate across the planet. In 2004, Mark Zuckerberg and a group of friends at Harvard University devised an innovative social networking platform that connected fellow students in an online community. Today, Facebook has more than 2.2 billion users worldwide.

From the early days of Bulletin Board Systems (BBS) to email to the phenomenon that is social networking, the internet is a communication tool like no other and it has radically changed the way we communicate. In the last two decades, our devices and their enabling technology have proven to be a boon to person-to-person communication, but it is also changing how we engage with and access services and entertainment. Throughout this book we'll talk about how emerging technologies and machine learning are now enabling communication not only between people, but between devices, and the impact that this will have on our daily lives. For now, let's concentrate on how we've used the Internet as a human-to-human communication tool in the near past.

Do you remember your first email account? Mine was a personal account with AOL (America Online). One of the early pioneers of the internet in the mid-1990s, AOL originally provided a dial-up service to millions of early adapters. Dial-up services allowed connectivity to the internet through a standard telephone line. Shortly thereafter, my company obtained our first business email address. Our professional address was a lengthy one — about 25 characters. At the time we had absolutely no idea how much we would come to use that email address. Email started as a kind of a novelty, with most business then being conducted in person, by telephone, or through the fax machine.

For most mainstream home users of the internet, the motivation to obtain a home computer was driven by the desire to communicate with friends and family via the convenience of email. The continual evolution of communication technologies means we can now send, receive, and archive emails from our smartphones as well as access other communication tools such as Facebook Messenger, Instagram, and Twitter, and text apps such as WhatsApp, WeChat, LINE, and Viber. These days, almost the last thing we use our smartphones for is as a telephone. FaceTime, Skype, Zoom, and other face-to-face video technologies enable us to connect across time and space in real-time conversations with anyone at any time.

3. The Internet As a Planning Tool

Partly because of their power to connect us to one another and partly because of their astonishing capacity to store and process data and information, computers and the internet have become the central pillars of personal and project planning. Over the last two decades we've come to rely on these tools in nearly every kind of business and industry. On the personal side, we use computers, laptops, tablets, smartphones and smartwatches to control our calendars, manage our money, shop, coordinate travel, and keep track of family and friends across the globe.

Leaving aside business and professional uses, can you imagine planning a family vacation without using the internet? What about booking service appointments, scheduling classes and leisure activities, or planning a party? Because internet use has become so completely integrated with the tasks of ordinary day-to-day life, we take for granted the scope of our reliance on it to support our basic needs and goals.

At this point it would be useful for you to take some time to assess your own (or your family's) internet use. It will help as you move toward making choices and decisions about increasing your commitment to learning about and integrating smart technologies into your daily life. Use Worksheet 1: Internet Use: Current Personal and Family Priorities to determine how much (or how little) you use the internet for research, planning, and communication now and how you anticipate using it in the future.

This kind of assessment will also help you identify your priorities. For example, perhaps you live in an area where home security is a major concern, or you have aging parents or relatives in your home who would like simplified internet access. Maybe you would like to streamline grocery shopping or meal planning? Working through a personal assessment should provide you with insight into what will work best for you and your family. It is the first step in making a simple and personalized plan for an integrated network. Keep in mind as you go, that the way you are using the internet today is not necessarily the way you will be using it tomorrow.

Worksheet 1
Internet Use: Current Personal and Family Priorities

Use this worksheet to understand the way you and your family are currently using the internet. We'll also refer to it later in the book to help determine whether or not you need more robust Wi-Fi in your home to support new Internet of Things technology.

	Family Member 1	Family Member 2	Family Member 3	Family Member 4
Name	Mom	Dad	Peter	Ellen
Research				
Evernote	☒	☐	☐	☐
Website bookmarks	☒	☐	☒	☒
Education accounts	☒	☐	☐	☒
YouTube	☐	☒	☒	☐
Recipes	☐	☒	☐	☐
Travel destinations	☒	☒	☐	☐
Major purchases	☒	☒	☐	☒
Other	☐	☐	☐	☐
Communication				
Contacts	☒	☐	☐	☒
Email	☒	☒	☒	☒
Messenger	☒	☒	☒	☒
WeChat	☐	☐	☒	☐
Viber	☐	☐	☒	☐
Smartphone	☒	☒	☒	☒
FaceTime	☒	☒	☒	☒
Skype/Zoom	☒	☐	☐	☒
Other	☐	☐	☐	☐
Planning				
Calendar	☒	☐	☐	☐
Travel booking accounts	☒	☒	☐	☐
Notifications and Reminders	☒	☐	☒	☒
Transportation options and reservations	☒	☒	☐	☐
Maps and directions	☒	☒	☐	☒
Other	☐	☐	☐	☐
Other Uses (list here)				
Note: Online entertainment and social media are covered in Worksheet 2.				
business laptop	☒	☐	☐	☐
	☐	☐	☐	☐
	☐	☐	☐	☐

4. Welcome to the Internet of Things

For many years, I've had the pleasure of writing a regular digital lifestyle column for my local newspaper, one of Canada's Black Press publications. In a column in the early spring of 2019, I wrote about "domotics." Domotics (from the Latin word "domus," meaning house) combines domus with robotics, and is the term used to describe all phases of smarthome technology. It is the process or set of tools and devices that make up a "smart" home, comprising information technology, microtechnology, and electronics, including sensors and controls that monitor and automate temperature, lighting, security systems, and much else.

A smart house is one where highly automated systems govern the functions listed above. The list doesn't stop there. The integration of these technologies goes beyond obvious tasks such as turning lights off and on at preprogrammed times or automatically adjusting air conditioning or heating. Highly advanced systems will allow us to monitor and inventory the foodstuffs in our fridges, track menus and meal plans, and routinely order groceries, for example.

Domotics is only one aspect of the Internet of Things. It is a good place to start as our homes are such an important element of our lives. The home is the center of family life. It provides sanctuary and comfort, and it is the place from which we launch the practical aspects of our lives — where we eat, sleep, relax, and prepare ourselves to go out into the world of work and engage with the demands of daily life. We also have some control in our homes, and we are able to decide for ourselves how much, or how little, we will augment our domestic lives with technology.

In an article for ThoughtCo, a leading online reference and education site, author Jackie Craven suggests that, "The smarthome systems might even ensure a continuously cleaned cat litter box or a house plant that is forever watered." ("Exploring Home Automation and Domotics," ThoughtCo.com, February 19, 2019.) Further, wearable sensors can monitor which members of the family are at home, and where they are, adjusting the home environment based on the needs and preferences of the wearer. We already commonly use such tracking devices to keep track of iPhones, keys, and pets.

How might this improve the lifestyle and safety of the elderly aging-in-place, or people with disabilities? Geofencing is being widely used in the IoT, creating virtual perimeters in real-world geographic areas, activating alerts or messages, triggered by location-based data.

Of course, many of our choices are dictated by the available technology. A rotary-dial phone is now only a collector's item. Telephone landlines are becoming a rarity, and data caps can limit smartphone use. Further, our personal choices are and will be limited (or expanded) by the positions taken by laws and regulations. For example, the introduction of emission controls on automobiles in the 1960s made certain kinds of car exhaust systems obsolete. The greening of the economy has forced automobile and other manufacturers to look for alternatives.

Social and economic trends, and changing legislation combined with advances in technology, can force consumer adaptation in the marketplace. The rise of electric propulsion fueled partly by government regulation and incentives is complemented by the increasing complexity of vehicles as environments for work and relaxation. Most of us are already using smart technology in our daily commute to make it more comfortable and time effective. We comfortably use the Global Positioning System (GPS) a satellite-based radio navigation system. Owned by the United States military, this is the technology that will enable driverless cars. Our cars are self-monitoring, notifying us when fuel or tires are low, or the engine needs servicing. Our smartphones are connected via Bluetooth to our car's audio systems, allowing us to personalize in-car entertainment, access the internet, and talk on our phones safely. We begin to take this kind of technology for granted soon after it is introduced.

Entertainment choices are already undergoing rapid change. For many, typical cable television is already obsolete, gone the way of the telephone landline. Known as cord-cutters, many television consumers are cancelling their cable accounts and moving to wholly internet TV-user apps such as Apple TV, Chromecast, or Amazon Fire TV. Live television streaming services such as Sling TV and DirecTV in the United States allow you to get most of your favorite stations streamed over the internet. Generally speaking, the fees are minimal compared to the average cable package and puts control of content in the hands of the consumer. Platforms such as Spotify and Apple Music make it possible to access millions of artists and playlists for a small monthly fee. Because of the IoT, you can listen to your favorite songs, podcasts, or radio programs on your smartphone, portable speakers, car, computer, or television set.

The world's libraries are at our fingertips via e-reader devices and apps. I believe that paper books will always be available, but the capacity to have thousands of books on hand without taking up space, and the convenience of ebook reading is unparalleled.

Machine learning, artificial intelligence (AI) and automation, virtual reality (VR) and augmented reality (AR) are all having a profound effect on entertainment and leisure options. As these technologies become more sophisticated, so will the experiences available in regard to gaming and other leisure experiences such as travel, sports, and shopping.

Given the public interest in consumer electronics for improving health (think about the popularity of Garmins, Fitbits, and the health apps in Apple Watches, for example), there has been a rapid development and incorporation of digital medical technologies into the health-care system. It is important to build digital health literacy for patients, community members, and health-care professionals to respond to the emerging opportunities. The implications of data-based, tailor-made diagnoses and treatments are profound, not just for personal medical or health-care choices, but in the potential reduction of health-care costs. These apps and technologies not only help patients manage their own health, they help health-care practitioners facilitate and improve patient care.

5. Summing Up

We live in a world where we can communicate directly with machine intelligence through our voices, gestures, or keypads. As our machines become more familiar with our preferences, their ability to keep us safe, comfortable, healthy, informed, and entertained grows ever more precise.

Through the rest of the book I'll cover available and pending IoT options in more detail, and provide you with insights, advice, tips, and exercises to help you better understand how the IoT can fit into your life.

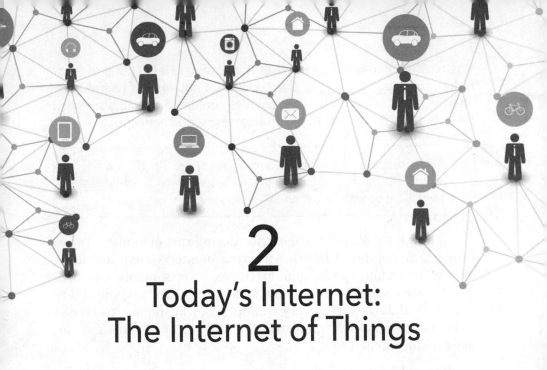

2
Today's Internet:
The Internet of Things

As discussed in the introduction, the average person navigating today's technology may feel as if he or she is entering a world of arcane and mysterious knowledge, accessible to only a few who understand its cryptic systems and terms. Fortunately, there are many resources that can help us decipher the terminology and understand this complex world. Technology experts abound and are generous in sharing insight and help.

I've leaned heavily on these resources in the upcoming chapter to offer you what I hope is an accessible definition of the IoT and how it works, as well as to introduce information about the networks needed to support the connected home.

1. What Is the Internet of Things and How Does It Work?

An invaluable online resource is WhatIs.com, TechTarget's IT encyclopedia and learning center. WhatIs.com is an award-winning website and is cited as an authority in such major publications as *The New York Times*, *Time*, *USA Today*, *The Washington Times*, *PC*, and *Discover*.

Written and managed by Margaret Rouse and a global team of technology experts, and part of the TechTarget network of technology-specific websites, WhatIs.com provides simple and straightforward definitions of thousands of technology terms and concepts.

> To find simple and straightforward definitions of the IoT or other technology terms and concepts, visit www.whatis.techtarget.com and type your term into the search bar.

So how does WhatIs.com describe the Internet of Things? It says, "The internet of things, or IoT, is a system of interrelated computing devices, mechanical and digital machines, objects, animals, or people that are provided with unique identifiers (UIDs) and the ability to transfer data over a network without requiring human-to-human or human-to-computer interaction." (More on why humans and animals are included in a bit.)

Unique Identifiers, or UIDs, are computer-speak for the alphanumeric or numeric address of an entity within a system. Think, for example, of the user ID or username you create when you register for a website or sign up for an online service. A website URL is another form of UID, and so are bank identifier codes (such as PIN codes) and product serial numbers. More common forms of UIDs are social security numbers, phone numbers, health-care numbers or patient codes, and email addresses.

In the IoT ecosystem, consisting of web-enabled smart devices, data is passed from address to address via embedded processors, sensors, and communication hardware. The devices can share the data because they are connected to the internet through a gateway. A gateway is a physical device or software program that serves as the connection point between the cloud and controllers, sensors and intelligent devices. The combination of a router and modem is a gateway.

That's a lot to take in, isn't it? Not to worry, we're going to dive into the practical applications of IoT technology and what it might mean for you and your family as we go, but let's first consider what might appear as a contradiction in the definition above. Central to the Internet of Things is the transferring of data from device to device without the requirement for human interaction. Nevertheless, people (and animals) are included in the definition as part of the "things." When we think about the word "thing" itself, it is an ambiguous and somewhat vague term used to define what cannot be specifically described. This means the scope for the application of the IoT is very broad indeed. Rouse explains it this way. "A thing in the internet of things can be a person with a heart monitor implant, a farm animal with a biochip transponder, an automobile that has built-in sensors to alert the driver when tire pressure is low or any other natural or man-made object that can be assigned an IP address and is able to transfer data over a network." The things in the IoT may be human, plant, animal, or machine, but subsequent to initial set-up, the network itself does not require human intervention because the technology is smart. Makes sense?

2. What Makes Smart Technology So Smart?

In a 2014 article in the *Harvard Business Review*, "How Smart, Connected Products Are Transforming Companies", Michael E. Porter and James E. Heppleman described three core elements that define the smart, connected devices we include under the umbrella term the Internet of Things. They are:

1. **Physical:** These are the mechanical and electrical components that comprise the product's parts, including the devices themselves. Your computer is a physical component of the system, as are speakers, routers, cables, and other hardware. It is what is inside — the microprocessors, chips, and software as described below — that make it smart.

2. **Smart:** These are the sensors, microprocessors, controls, software, and data storage components that enable advanced functionality. Typically, the smart components include a user interface — the means by which the you and the computer system interact — and an embedded operating system or apps — the configurations of which are designed so that the device performs a specific task or function and learns from the data it gathers.

3. **Connectivity:** These are the antennae, ports, and protocols that enable wired or wireless connections with the product, not only to the internet or the cloud, but also to other systems and devices. This allows the information and data to be exchanged.

What is important about the distinctions made by Porter and Heppelmann is, first, that they help to clarify the complex set of systems and relationships that make the IoT possible. They are also making it clear that "smart" and connected are not the same thing. A device can be connected to the internet and not be smart. What makes a product, device, or a component of a product or device smart is its ability to gather data and analyze it, and then take logical actions based on the analysis. As the aforementioned definition suggests, all this occurs without requiring human-to-human or human-to-computer interaction. The products function in an independent way. Products which are smart and connected offer a set of functions and capabilities that can be grouped into four areas: monitoring, control, optimization, and autonomy.

1. **Monitoring:** Using sensors and external data sources, a smart connected product can track internal and external conditions and alert users to changes in performance or circumstances. Think of an ECG (electrocardiogram) for example. Sensors monitor heart rate and activity and display the activity as a series of peaks and dips on a screen. This provides information about the state of a patient's heart. Medical monitors can also produce alarms alerting medical staff of significant changes. In the case of a pacemaker, a small electrical charge may be administered to properly regulate heartbeat. Similarly, in your home a smart thermostat monitors the environment and makes minor temperature adjustments to maintain comfort.

2. **Control:** Products are controlled through remote commands or algorithms (a process or rules that direct a specific computer response) that allow the users to personalize their interaction with the product — for example turning "smart" lights off and on at specified times using a smartphone, or operating home security cameras or door locks remotely.

3. **Optimization:** As smart, connected products and devices gather usage data, analytics can be applied to improve and optimize product performance. This can have a dramatic effect not only on utilization and efficiency, but also on streamlining user preferences and personalization. Machines "learn" our habits and optimize accordingly.

4. **Autonomy:** According to Porter and Heppelmann, one of the simplest examples of autonomous product operation is the iRobot Roomba, a vacuum cleaner that uses sensors and software to clean floors. Because devices are capable of sophisticated monitoring, controlling, and optimizing, they can learn about their environment, respond to patterns, diagnose needs, adapt preferences, and ultimately make choices.

My friend and technology expert Steve Dotto suggests we add "focus" to the list above, in that smart devices typically do only one thing, but they do it very well. Stacey Higginbotham, technology expert, and editor of *Stacey on the IoT*, a technology news website and companion podcast, offers a clarifying perspective that just because a thing is connected to the Internet that doesn't make it an IoT device. While printers and computers connect to the Internet, they are not necessarily smart. Says Higginbotham, "an IoT device or a 'smart' device is one that connects to a network, gathers data, and then uses that data to provide insights or take an automated action. "

This definition is consistent with the distinctions described above by Porter and Heppelman. Further, says Higginbotham in her October 2019 article, "There are Three Different Versions of the IoT," "Consumer IoT devices need an interface via an app, website, or screen on the device; they should moreover provide a service as opposed to simply remote access. (I suppose the ability to turn down my thermostat from my couch is a service, but I want to see the data gathered by the device put to use.) So a Wi-Fi-connected oven that I can turn on or preheat from an app isn't really consumer IoT unless it also has the ability to gauge my food's temperature in order to better cook it, or if it can share its energy consumption data with the grid to help adjust the demand for energy in my home or in my neighborhood."

By now you have a basic grasp of what separates a smart device from a "dumb" one and the components or elements that make the Internet of Things possible. This brave new world is possible because of a combination of microtechnology, applied machine learning, artificial intelligence, robotics, and, as we discussed in Chapter 1, the application of these technologies in our homes, known as domotics. Throughout the rest of the book I'll discuss various devices, platforms, products, apps, and technologies that you are most likely to come across as you think about your network. Not all of these will fall strictly into the definitions provided above, but let's use the definitions as guideposts.

As a consumer, you do not need to have a comprehensive grasp of the distinctions delineated by these definitions, nor be a technology wizard in order to engage with smart (or even partially smart) devices, but it is helpful to have the basics. My aim is to increase your general understanding of the Internet of Things and introduce at least some of the myriad possibilities available to you in your day-to-day life.

Before we go too much further, it will be helpful to explore a few other key concepts that will be useful, in the following sections.

3. Let's Talk Networks

It is not necessary that you fully understand the many layers of enabling technology involved in the world of the IoT in order to use it, but I will cover the basics of the three main components introduced earlier in the chapter: the physical components, the smart components, and the connectivity components. In later chapters I'll go into some detail about the popular smart devices, platforms, and programs that make up the physical world of the IoT, but for now let's talk networks: The place where the connectivity magic happens.

Most readers will be comfortably familiar with Wi-Fi. (Although some of you, depending on your age or location, may have a PC "wired in" at home, or may even be hanging on to dial-up internet.) If you happen to drive a newer car, you likely also have an acquaintance with Bluetooth, the frequency standard that pairs your smartphone with your car's speaker and entertainment system.

It may be helpful to think of standards like Bluetooth as languages. In the simplest terms, the IoT commonly speaks four: Wi-Fi, Bluetooth, ZigBee, and Z-Wave. These are the standards, or protocols, by which our devices communicate. These are the various paths traveled by data and information as it moves from device to device, creating a network. Networks connect to platforms — the basic hardware and software on which applications run — but it is important to remember that not every platform supports every technology. Let's take a look at each of these network protocols.

3.1 Wi-Fi

Wi-Fi uses radio waves to transfer data from the internet across networks. For most home networks it is the modem that connects to the internet and a router that connects various devices to Wi-Fi. These days, most routers and modems come bundled in one device called a gateway. Depending on your Internet Service Provider (ISP) this equipment will be provided to you free of charge as part of your service, it might be rented as part of a contract, or you can purchase your own.

In an interview for this book, Don Lekei, the founder and owner of Help-My-Tech and an in-home tech expert, advised that one of the first things to ensure, before deciding to add smarthome devices to your network, is that your Wi-Fi is robust enough to handle your needs. Most consumer-grade Wi-Fi will effectively handle a handful of smart devices without too much trouble. Depending on your family's device use and how comprehensive your system is, however, you may want to consider a dedicated Wi-Fi router for your smarthome setup. In some ways routers/gateways are like cars; there are economy models and luxury models. If you have a lot of traffic in your home system, you may want to invest in a more deluxe version to manage your Wi-Fi.

In addition to thinking about the scope and nature of device use in your home, another consideration is the range and speed of your Wi-Fi. Most commercial Wi-Fi frequencies are either 2.4 GHz or 5 GHz (most newer routers are dual-bands which include both). In very simplified terms, a 2.4 GHz is a more congested frequency but will give you more range, while a 5 GHz network will be faster as it is a less crowded frequency, but devices will work more effectively closer to the router.

Typically, you can find out the bandwidth of your router on the label attached to the side or bottom of the device. If you purchased your equipment yourself, this information will be on the product box or included in the installation instructions. You can also look up your equipment specifications online. You will need this information as you consider the bandwidth needs of your devices. For example, a smart thermostat or smart plug will be fine using 2.4 GHz, (in fact some products will only work on 2.4 GHz) while streaming and gaming will likely need a speedier connection. In setting up my own smart plug system, I found my specific Internet Service Provider's (ISP) online help desk very useful. I have a dual-band router but both bands shared one name (SSID). This made it difficult for those devices that only use the 2.4 GHz frequency to find the right frequency automatically. With the help desk agent's guidance, I was able to give each of my frequencies their own name and set up my 2.4 GHz smart plugs very quickly.

In many homes, Wi-Fi range is an issue. It can be challenging to get fast and reliable Wi-Fi into every nook and cranny. Large appliances, other technology, and architecture can all affect the ability of the Wi-Fi signal to travel through the home. Wi-Fi boosters or repeaters are devices that can extend and amplify the Wi-Fi signal. In general, consumer Wi-Fi extenders are universal and will work with the majority of wireless routers. Frequencies, as described above, apply to these devices as well. If your equipment comes from an Internet Service Provider as part of a contract, many also offer proprietary extender packs that can be added.

3.2 Mesh networking

Unlike a series of Wi-Fi boosters or extenders which are repeating the Wi-Fi signal throughout the network, a mesh network acts as an independent self-contained network where one point links to the modem and acts as the router, while the other devices (or nodes) within the network capture the router's signal and rebroadcast it. Rather than have devices connect to a central access point, they connect to each other. Typically, mesh networks run on the Bluetooth, ZigBee, or Z-Wave standards which are described below.

3.3 Bluetooth

Bluetooth is essentially a wireless short-link radio technology for exchanging data between fixed and mobile devices over short distances. You are likely to be most familiar with Bluetooth wireless headphones or headsets, or as the technology that pairs your smartphone with your car's audio or display control system. Bluetooth has become the auto-industry standard for hands-free mobile use, pairing your phone with the smart technology found in newer cars. Bluetooth technology is also used in mesh networks that support common smarthome applications such as lights, HVAC systems, door locks, and smart white goods like washers, dryers, and refrigerators. Even though using the internet and Wi-Fi to connect smart devices generally works, there are issues related to the range of Wi-Fi, congested bandwidth, and energy consumption. Bluetooth addresses these issues by offering a short-range alternate pathway. Typically, when setting up your smart devices, you will be asked to enable Bluetooth as well.

3.4 ZigBee and Z-Wave

In order to be truly efficient, smart devices have to communicate with each other. As consumers, we want simple-to-use, safe systems that make our lives easier. As we noted in Chapter 1, aside from security and privacy concerns, one of the main challenges with the networked home and smart technology is the lack of standardized protocols or standards for connectivity and interoperability between devices, especially those that aren't native to one another — all Apple, all Google, or all Amazon, for example.

ZigBee and Z-Wave are the two most common standards for smart devices that offer low-power, low-bandwidth protocols. They require some kind of dedicated hub, such as Amazon's Alexa. Most ZigBee and Z-Wave devices are generally compatible with Apple Homepod, Alexa, and Google Home. They come built into hubs like Hubitat and Samsung's SmartThings. (We'll talk more about hubs in Chapter 4.)

As you shop for devices, get in the habit of checking the boxes or asking staff for information about compatibility, required bandwidth, and network standards. ZigBee and Z-Wave do connect to Wi-Fi but require a bridge to do so.

Use Worksheet 2 to learn about whether your Wi-Fi is working well for your family's needs.

4. A Few Resources

In addition to the information offered by websites such WhatIs.com there are many resources available online to help you navigate and understand the IoT and the networks that support it. I found the online tutorials offered by Steve Cope very helpful in understanding networking basics for smarthomes and home automation. You can find Steve's Smarthome Guide here: stevessmarthomeguide.com. Matt Ferrell also has an excellent six-episode YouTube series called *Smarthome for Beginners* on his channel Undecided.

If you are interested in technology in general, please check out the work of my colleague Steve Dotto of DottoTech. His funny, accessible, and insightful YouTube channel and webinar series are enjoyed the world over. You can find him at dottotech.com

Worksheet 2
The Scope and Scale of In-Home Wi-Fi Use and Family Entertainment

Online Entertainment and Social Media				
	Family Member 1	Family Member 2	Family Member 3	Family Member 4
Name	Mom	Dad	Peter	Ellen
Facebook	☒	☐	☒	☒
Twitter	☒	☐	☒	☐
Instagram	☒	☐	☒	☒
LinkedIn	☒	☐	☐	☒
Snapchat	☐	☐	☒	☐
TikTok	☐	☐	☒	☐
WhatsApp	☐	☐	☒	☐
Gaming	☐	☒	☒	☒
Participation in online chat threads or groups	☒	☒	☒	☒
Online shopping	☒	☒	☐	☒
YouTube	☒	☒	☒	☐
Movie and TV streaming	☐	☒	☒	☒
Other				
Fitness	☒	☒	☒	☐
	☐	☐	☐	☐
	☐	☐	☐	☐

Now that you have this information, let's break it down and see how your systems are functioning for your family. Refer to Worksheet 1 to help identify the way different family members use the internet.

Family Member 1	Mom
Primary internet use	work, social connection
Devices used	tablet, smartphone, TV
Typical location in home	office, living room
Satisfaction with Wi-Fi performance: (1 not at all, 5 completely)	☐ 1 ☐ 2 ☐ 3 ☒ 4 ☐ 5

Worksheet 2 – Continued

Family Member 2	Dad
Primary internet use	research, recipes, fitness, TV
Devices used	tablet, smartphone, TV
Typical location in home	kitchen, living room
Satisfaction with Wi-Fi performance: (1 not at all, 5 completely)	☐ 1 ☐ 2 ☐ 3 ☒ 4 ☐ 5

Family Member 3	Peter
Primary internet use	social media, gaming, TV
Devices used	phone, laptop, TV, tablet
Typical location in home	bedroom, living room
Satisfaction with Wi-Fi performance: (1 not at all, 5 completely)	☐ 1 ☒ 2 ☐ 3 ☐ 4 ☐ 5

Family Member 4	Ellen
Primary internet use	research for school, social contact
Devices used	laptop, tablet, phone
Typical location in home	bedroom, living room, kitchen
Satisfaction with Wi-Fi performance: (1 not at all, 5 completely)	☐ 1 ☐ 2 ☒ 3 ☐ 4 ☐ 5

If your overall rating is poor for Wi-Fi performance in a given area of your home, consider checking the frequencies and adjusting them, installing a repeater, or upgrading your router as described in Chapter 2, section 3.1. If you are unsatisfied with your Wi-Fi performance at this level of internet use, you will need to make it more robust in order to support IoT technology.

*Use additional paper or duplicate this worksheet if you have additional family members.

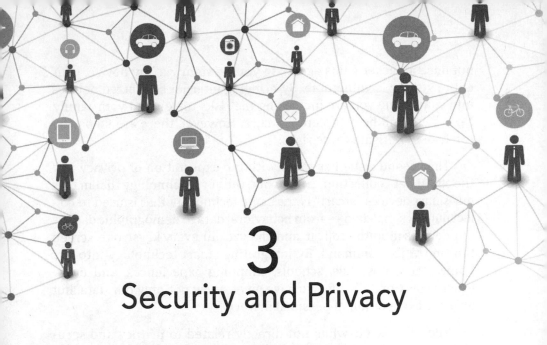

3
Security and Privacy

Now that you have a basic understanding of how the IoT works, let's address the considerable concerns about data and privacy, as well as the overall security of integrated systems.

As you consider the options for the integration of the IoT into your daily life, security and privacy concerns are paramount. Computer hacking is a very real concern. From neighborhood kids with savvy tech skills hacking into your system to take it for a joyride, to organized crime networks with teams of hackers looking for open doorways to tangible assets, our home computers and interconnected systems are vulnerable.

There are three main issues to consider as you make your choices around networked systems. The first has to do with cybersecurity and the potential threats posed by cyber criminals or cyber vandals. It is not just devices such as laptops, smartphones, and tablets that are vulnerable. Household security cameras, smart speakers, and smart lightbulbs can be hacked. While it may simply be creepy to think about a stranger taking a peek at you while you are watching your smart TV, it may be a different matter entirely to have them watching your children sleep via the baby monitor. Not only that, but once a hacker gains access to your system via any device, your entire system is vulnerable. By bringing internet connected devices into your home you are increasing the risks to you and your family. No system will be completely secure. However, there are steps you can take to mitigate these risks.

The second issue has to do with the expectation of privacy and the age of data collection. Simply put, the very technology that makes our smart devices "smart" is the same technology that is used to collect our personal data — from behavioral data to demographic data — our devices monitor, collect, and analyze our every keystroke, screen tap, and voice command. By integrating smart technology into our homes, cars, hospitals, schools, shopping experiences, and every other aspect of daily life, we have given away not only our data, but also our expectation of personal privacy.

The third issue, while not directly related to privacy and security concerns, is a kind of cousin to them. As with all technology related matters, we are in a fast-moving, ever-evolving world. In the introduction to this book, I made the point that there is still some distance to go in terms of efficient and affordable, fully networked systems. The tools and protocols are not yet standardized to enable devices with different vendor origins to communicate effectively. The sophisticated networks required to run simple, affordable, easy-to-manage systems are not in place yet. This creates a challenge for typical consumers and also contributes to problems with secure encryption, and added system vulnerability.

1. The Right to Privacy

It is natural to have an expectation of privacy, especially in typical North American or Western European cultures where personal privacy is seen as a cornerstone of democracy. Varonis, a leading worldwide cybersecurity company, had this to say in an August 18, 2019, article about data security and privacy: "Privacy is the right of an individual to be free from uninvited surveillance. To safely exist in one's space and freely express one's opinion behind closed doors is critical to living in a democratic society." (www.varonis.com/blog/data-privacy, accessed December 2019.) The article goes on to quote Dr. Ann Cavoukian, former Information and Privacy Commissioner of Ontario, Canada, who says, "Privacy forms the basis of our freedom. You have to have moments of reserve, reflection, intimacy, and solitude."

Both in terms of the personal privacy — the right to live our lives as we see fit behind closed doors — and the right to know and understand what is being done with our behavioral data, the Internet of Things is problematic. Personal data is continually being collected, stored, and analyzed.

2. How Is Data Used?

You may be asking yourself: What is the point of all this data collection? First and foremost, from the point of view of the Internet of Things, data is the input that feeds machine learning. Machine learning draws on information produced by algorithms and statistics that are based on data extracted from, and produced by, multiple sources. Sources include location tracking apps, social media feeds, internet browsing, Google searches, security camera feeds, and nearly all the apps we download and use on our smartphones. Machine learning makes use of the algorithms to learn new tasks by making inferences from the data. At a basic level, the data from your browsing history alone can tell the algorithms who you are, where you've been, who you've been talking to, and what you're interested in.

Artificial Intelligence (AI) is the application of machine learning used to produce solutions, processes, and logical sequences. It is the data that is gathered as we engage and interact with our devices and internet-enabled objects that allows sophisticated algorithms to determine our preferences, habits, and tendencies. It is data that makes smart technology smart. It is also what has made empires for companies such as Google, Facebook, Apple, and Amazon.

There is enormous value to businesses in collecting, sharing, and using consumer data. How businesses and product manufacturers request consent, abide by privacy policies, and manage and store data is not always transparent. Few consumers take the trouble to read or understand opt-in agreements when signing up for a new service. In nearly all cases we are agreeing to having our usage data collected, stored, sold, or shared.

While many companies use the data they gather to refine and improve customer service, as consumers we must be wary of their motives. As an example, giving your genetic code to the internet, as promoted by ancestry research platforms, is probably not a good idea, even if you believe the data might be used for a beneficial cause, such as drug research. There simply aren't enough legal safeguards in place to protect your DNA and the ways it might be used by pharmaceutical companies or hackers.

My friend Fred Armstrong, Manager of Community Engagement for a small city, frames his concerns this way: "I have significant concerns that the information that I'm sending to tech companies is being used primarily to market products to me and not to improve the technology. We have seen repeated examples of how tech companies are morally bankrupt when it comes to the 'harm' that their tech brings to society. They do not think through the impacts of new tech, or if they do, they are ignoring the implications. The Internet of Things has enormous potential for humanity. The people that run these companies are not driven by innovation; they are driven by high earnings. This has been the most disappointing thing about the growth of the tech industry in my lifetime."

These fears and concerns can be balanced with the many good uses data is put to. Because Google knows where you are and how long it takes you to get from point A to point B, the data can be used to help you, and the many other motorists on the roads, avoid congestion, for example. Google Maps are used with confidence throughout the world and the continual improvement of the service is based on data. So, there is some evidence that the tech sector is responding to concerns about data collection and its uses, but as consumers we must be vigilant.

3. Data Security

We expect the manufacturers and retailers of technology products to respect our privacy and, if we've provided consent, to keep our data secure. It is important to understand the distinction between these. Data privacy governs how data is collected, shared, and used. Data security means keeping that collected data secure from compromise by external hackers, or to protect it from those inside the governing company or organization who may be dishonest. Data may be properly encrypted and monitored; however, if it is collected without consent, that may be a breach of privacy. This is a critical issue. How many consumers know what data the devices we bring into our homes, cars, and workplaces are gathering, or how this data is being used?

Worldwide, privacy and collection regulations are expanding, and requirements and regulations are changing. However, compliance varies from company to company and from country to country.

Legislative and regulatory standards are evolving, and mistakes have been, and will continue to be, made. So, what can you do to safeguard your privacy, and ensure your systems are secure?

4. The (In)Security of Home Networks

John Biehler, Editorial Director of GetConnected Media, and a leading Canadian technology journalist, kindly agreed to be interviewed for this book. His main concern in regard to the IoT has to do with privacy and security. "The Internet of Things, " he says, "is a minefield of potential security issues."

His concern is twofold. First, many manufacturers and developers of new products for home use are lazy, eager to get products to market quickly, and make it easy for the consumer to access the technology and set it up. While there are some simple things that the manufacturers could do to ensure, for example, that the webcam that is going to be set up in a baby's room is secure, they're not necessarily doing so. The second concern is consumers themselves. In the interest of simplicity, most of us will use the default passwords that come with the equipment, or if it's not strictly required, use no password at all.

A good example is the Wi-Fi router. Many people simply use the password that was given to them by the service provider, or use the one that or is written in the manual or on the box the equipment came in. This makes for simple set up, and creates a good customer experience, but it is highly insecure. Biehler points out that in a way these default passwords are "shared knowledge." Those who are tech savvy know what they are.

Manufacturers, suggests Biehler, could force consumers to change passwords before activating the equipment. Without a mechanism in place to force the new user to change the password, the system is vulnerable.

"All it takes is for a hacker to get into one of your devices, " says Biehler, "and they have access to your whole home network. Hackers can be monitoring what you are typing, what websites you visit, your bank account, tax information — basically it is as though they are sitting beside you as you go through your day-to-day activities online. And they are an uninvited guest."

This kind of vulnerability is not limited to your Wi-Fi router. Any smart device that you bring into your home has to be set up and configured, usually with a password, whether it's an app or a device such as Alexa or Google Home. Each of these points becomes what is known as an "attack vector," a potential place where people get lazy or where manufacturers or developers don't enforce rules of changing the defaults when installing. While it may sound like a plot lifted from a spy novel of yesteryear, hackers can infiltrate home networks through smart lightbulbs, smart toys, or smart appliances. They can spy on you and your family through your security cameras, smart speakers, or baby monitors, and they can spy on your data. Any type of device that has an internet connection can be hacked. Spying, stealing your privacy, and access to private information is one level of hacking. Another level is where hackers can reconfigure your passwords and take control of your home and your accounts.

Setting up and maintaining your smart life can be costly. Technology is expensive with a typical smartphone alone running into the hundreds, if not thousands, of dollars.

Often, consumers are looking to get a better deal or a more cost-effective product. This can create another area of concern in regard to privacy and security. Typically, cheaper products tend to be less secure. While devices manufactured and distributed by the Google, Apple, or Amazon brands will carry a higher price tag than products from lesser known brands, choosing a device or product from a major manufacturer makes more sense from a security perspective. These products are more likely to have greater initial installation safeguards in place as well as offer regular firmware updates.

Firmware is data that is stored on a device's ROM (read-only memory) that provides instruction on how that device should operate. Unlike software, firmware cannot be changed or deleted by a user without the aid of special programs. Firmware remains on the device whether the device is activated or not. Firmware updates are software programs that enhance the device's capabilities or fix problems or "bugs." Quite often, the problems are security holes and the updates act as patches, fixing these holes, and making the product more secure. Third-party updates are generally not supported by the product's manufacturer, which in part is why it is a safer bet to invest in equipment from well-known, established brands. This argument also holds true for smartphone updates. As the smartphone is very often the hub, or central brain, that governs the Internet of Things network, regularly downloading updates on your phone will also help to keep your system more secure.

Three key areas for concern when it comes to your system's privacy and security are: lax installation procedures, weak passwords, and cheaply manufactured downmarket products. To mitigate your risk: Replace the original product password with a strong and unique password at the outset and then change it regularly; buy products from reputable, established brands; and regularly download updates as they become available. No system will be completely safe. Understanding this, do what you can to make yours less vulnerable.

4.1 How to create a strong password

Every password should be unique. As I've already noted, do not continue to use the default password that came with your device or product. Do not use obvious or easily guessed passwords such as "password" or " 1234." Use a combination of upper and lower-case letters, special characters such as & * $ #, and one or more numbers. Use these combinations in unconventional patterns, for example capitalize the third rather than the obvious first letter of an alphanumeric password. Avoid using personal identifiers such as your last name, first name, birth date, street name, or address.

Most importantly, all accounts should have separate passwords. Keeping track of multiple, unique passwords can be time-consuming and troublesome, but it is well worth the time, particularly as the number of smart, connected devices in our lives grow. Another useful tip for safeguarding your systems is to use multiple email addresses. You may have a main personal or family email that you use for correspondence and accounts that are not a target for hackers, but use a different email address for personal banking, online shopping, or accessing medical records. A third address could be one you use for setting up your in-home IoT systems. A great resource for managing multiple email accounts using Gmail can be found in this YouTube video by Steve Dotto of DottoTech: www.youtube.com/watch?v=qQTwSYQX5tw.

> In Chapter 6 of my recent book, *Digital Legacy Plan, A Guide to the Personal and Practical Elements of Your Digital Life Before You Die* (Self-Counsel Press 2018) cowritten with Angela Crocker, I offer insight into the use of password managers and advice on password storage and record-keeping. It is available at www.self-counsel.com/digital-legacy-plan.html.

5. The Need for Standardization

Moving forward, we must become more aware of the risks of using IoT products in our homes, cars, and public spaces. We need to understand the nature of data collection and how it used and what that means in terms of our expectation of personal privacy. As well, we must confront the reality that while these systems are more sophisticated than we are, many are flawed and nearly all are in a constant state of development and redevelopment. Despite efforts to regulate and standardize, the world of the IoT is still very much the wild west. For the average consumer, setting up and managing smart technology at home can be a challenge in and of itself. Ensuring that these systems are secure and that privacy is protected adds an additional layer of complexity that manufacturers are only beginning to address.

It is not just a lack of tech savvy on the part of the average consumer that creates vulnerability (and frustration). The tech industry needs to step up and create networks, systems, and devices that address the issues of cost, complexity, and security. In her August 2019 online article, "There are 3 Different Versions of the IoT," (staceyoniot.com/there-are-3-different-versions-of-the-iot, accessed December 2019), Stacey Higginbotham notes that "Consumer IoT has unique challenges that companies need to address. For example, consumers have relatively unsophisticated networks, so getting devices online should be easy. The traffic between the devices and the Internet should also be encrypted because consumers aren't savvy when it comes to data protection. Given the number of potential connected devices in the consumer home, we're probably going to need robust networks — consumers will need hubs to handle translations between networks, which add cost and complexity. Consumer IoT needs to be built securely, with network redundancy, and at a low cost."

Higginbotham points out in the same article, that consumer IoT devices do not necessarily need to have a long shelf life — she estimates anywhere from three to ten years for most products — so that as the technology advances, products can become more streamlined and standardized. While efforts are being made in this area, there is still some distance to go before mainstream consumer IoT products are fully secure and simple to install and use. In subsequent chapters I'll offer some insight and advice to consumers in making smart personal IoT choices.

The final words in this section go to John Biehler: "If people have accepted the trade-off between security and convenience and accepted the risks and at least understand what they are getting into, it can be a great time to be alive. We are living the future where enabling technology can make our lives easier."

But, as technology experts like Biehler remind us, it is ultimately a trade-off. We are trading security and the expectation of privacy for the potential convenience and ease of using products to streamline our day-to-day activities. Only you can decide if the trade-off is a worthwhile one. Worksheet 3 will help you determine your own comfort level.

Worksheet 3

Privacy and You: How Comfortable Are You with Data Sharing?

Questions	Yes	No
Do you carry a smartphone?	☒	☐
Do you use your phone's built-in voice assistant?	☒	☐
Do you use GPS in your car or Google (or other) Maps on your phone?	☒	☐
Do you have accounts on and engage on the common social media platforms?	☒	☐
Do you wear a fitness tracker, or a smartwatch?	☒	☐
Do you use social media messaging services?	☒	☐
Have you read the Terms of Service agreements related to your networked devices, apps, and platforms?	☐	☒
Do you order products or schedule services online?	☒	☐
Do you use either default passwords or simple passwords that are similar to each other and therefore easy to remember?	☐	☒

If you answered yes to most of the questions above, you are already sharing a great deal of data about yourself including where you live, driving and travel habits, shopping and product preferences as well as much more. Remember, no system is truly private and secure.

Keeping in mind that you are probably already sharing a great deal of data online, reflect on the following questions to determine whether you are ready to provide more data in exchange for the convenience of Internet of Things technology.

☐ Yes, I am willing to share my personal data.

☒ Yes, I am willing to share my personal data if it benefits others (e.g., health research).

☒ Yes, I am willing to share my data if it benefits me (e.g., app discounts, reductions in insurance premiums).

☒ Yes, I am willing to share my data if it is the only way I can access an app or online service.

☐ Yes, I am willing to share my data if it will improve services to me or others (e.g., improved voice recognition).

☐ No, but I feel resigned to it if I am to access apps and services.

☐ No, I am not willing to share data.

4
Connected Home: The Devices

Many of us are already employing smart technologies as part of a regular domestic routine. You probably have a smart thermostat, or a garage door that will automatically close. Does your coffeepot come on at a prescheduled time in the morning? Have you had a security system installed with cameras or sensors that monitor movement or the opened or closed status of windows or doors? These are examples of embedded smart technology, or at least of sophisticated automation. Many of us have been using technology to automate aspects of our homes for years, often relying on specialists such as home security companies, or garage door installers to mount the required systems and demonstrate how to use them. What's changed is not only the sheer number of "things" that have become smart and the ability to network them together, but also the consumer appetite for DIY (Do It Yourself) technology solutions.

Rob Richardson is Senior National Account Manager for Arlo Technologies, a global home automation company that makes wireless security cameras. Richardson manages the Canadian retail side of the business and kindly agreed to be interviewed for this book. In our interview, we talked about how our expectations in regard to home technology have changed.

As Richardson explained, the wireless age began with the invention and release of wireless routers to consumers around 1997. They were exciting but relatively low-power. The exciting part was that for the first time you could sit at your kitchen table with your computer not plugged in, and get internet.

Said Richardson, "It was revolutionary, but never in a million years did we have the expectation that we could lie in our bedrooms upstairs and have the internet without being wired in. The only way you could do that was to run internet cable throughout your home which became the thing in home building 15 or so years ago. Fast forward to better routers, and then we could go from our kitchen tables to our living room couch. The technology got a little better and a little better, but we still had dead spots, places in our homes without internet. Continue to fast forward to today we have the expectation for what is termed whole home Wi-Fi. No dead spots, and access everywhere 24/7."

Richardson credits both the rise of smartphone use and the introduction of Netflix into the marketplace as key drivers for these expectations. Using smartphones meant we needed to be connected, and because the technology was all about being mobile, we needed to be connected everywhere. Netflix subscribers started buying iPads and other tablets. The price of flat screen TVs came way down. Streaming services expanded. Today, it is not uncommon for our homes to have several flat screen TVs, numerous smartphones, and a variety of personal computers, laptops, and tablets. Thus, the demand for Wi-Fi throughout the home. The technology marketplace responded with better, faster routers, Wi-Fi boosters and range extenders, and mesh networks. These devices are what make our smarthomes possible and are the enabling technologies that support the Internet of Things.

In 2014, the online shopping giant Amazon introduced Alexa, a virtual assistant embedded in a smart speaker. Today, smart speaker sales are booming, and double-digit growth is expected over the next five years in in home network hubs such as Amazon's Echo or Google Home. At the time of this writing, according to Statista, an international provider of market and consumer data, an estimated 35 percent of US households are equipped with at least one smart speaker. They forecast that by 2025 this will increase to around 75 percent. A November 2019 article in iotforall.com, "IoT In 2020: 5 Things You Need To Know," predicts, "An increasing number of IoT cameras, appliances and sensors are used every year, and 2020 will continue the steady pace of growth. A new forecast from International Data Corporation estimates that, by 2025, there will be over 41 billion connected devices generating 80 zettabytes of data." These staggering numbers mean that not only will smart devices be ubiquitous, but because of access to such vast quantities of data they will be getting ever smarter.

In this chapter, we'll discuss what to consider and how to identify your family's in-home needs and preferences in choosing the devices to control your connected life. As noted in the introduction, our homes are our sanctuaries. We want our private environments to be happy, safe, and healthy ones. As with choosing any system, personal preference will play a key role, as will the individual user needs in your home. In choosing smart devices for your home it is important that they enhance your quality of life by offering more convenience, ease, or simplification.

In the preceding chapters, we discussed the implications of "going smart" at home in terms of privacy and security, and we covered the basics in regard to the technology itself: what makes it smart and how it runs. One of the main issues concerning installing and maintaining smart gadgets at home is getting them to work together. For the non tech-savvy, this can be difficult and frustrating. The lack of standards and the proprietary nature of existing protocols means that products from one manufacturer to another often fail to work together. There is no doubt that as time goes by and technology companies invest more and more in ensuring a positive consumer experience, systems and gadgets will become more streamlined, more secure, and simpler to install and use. Having said that, from smartphones to smart cars, interconnected devices are a pervasive part of daily life already. The fact that you are reading this book suggests that you have already, or are about to, investigate adding smart technology to your home. So, let's take a look at some of the more common devices that are available that may enhance your life at home.

1. All about the Smartphone

The smartphone is the hub or central brain that enables integration with the various apps, devices, and objects that make up the personal IoT network. It is the heart of the conversation between the things. This is not to confuse the smartphone as hub with the kind of hub or smart speaker device that may be used to coordinate signals amongst other devices, such as Amazon Echo, Google Home, or Apple's HomePod, or with the kind of bridge or gateway hub that may be needed to have devices work together. We will go into those in more detail in this section. Depending on your needs and choices a smartphone and suitable Wi-Fi may be all you need to set up and manage effective smart systems in your home at this time.

For the purposes of the IoT, think of the smartphone as a sophisticated form of remote control, similar to a television clicker. There are two primary operating systems used in mobile technology — Google's Android and Apple's iOS. Android is used by many different phone manufacturers and is the world's most commonly used smartphone platform, while iOS is used only on Apple devices.

No doubt your particular smartphone is already equipped with a variety of useful and time-saving apps based on your particular operating system. As you begin to set up and/or manage your networked life, these and other apps will play an important role. You will need to install companion apps related to your smart devices as part of your connected home.

From your smartphone or tablet you can control a multitude of home functions: TVs, speakers, lights, switches, outlets, thermostats, windows, fans, air conditioners, humidifiers, air purifiers, sensors, security, locks, cameras, doorbells, and garage doors. Add to this list "life management" tasks such as timers, reminders, appointment scheduling, phone calls, recipes — yes, there's an app for all of that!

Typically, you will need to create an account with the app and connect it to your Wi-Fi. As well, through the remote function of your phone, you can control the additional bridges or other hubs you may need to make your system work most effectively. The use of your smartphone as control central is not limited to your home systems. Through Bluetooth technology your smartphone will pair with navigation and entertainment apps in your smart car. As well, travel and transportation apps, shopping apps, and health-monitoring systems can all be installed and managed on your phone.

2. Voice Assistants

The app functions described above can be controlled by a simple tap. You can also control many functions on your phone via voice activation.

There are three common digital voice-activated systems in the marketplace today — Apple's Siri, Amazon's Alexa, and Google's Google Assistant. It is predicted that voice activation will continue to grow as new applications for these services emerge. Not only is the technology improving — voice recognition software has become more accurate, able to distinguish between individual voices and tell the difference between human voice and machine voice — but consumers are becoming more comfortable interacting with voice assistants and the artificial intelligence that governs them. Let's meet today's most familiar virtual assistants.

2.1 Meet Siri

My colleague, author Angela Crocker, teaches digital marketing at a well-known technical trade college in Canada. One of the first demonstrations she does with new classes each semester involves Crocker calling out "Hey, Siri" from the front of the classroom. Without fail at least a third of the students' phones ping and respond, "Can I help" or "I'm listening." Crocker uses the demonstration as part of a lesson on optimizing internet search, including voice-activated search.

Siri is a built-in, voice-controlled personal virtual assistant (VA) for Apple iPhone users. It is available not only on the iPhone but also iPad, Apple Watch, iPod Touch, AirPods and HomePod. We'll talk more about devices such as HomePod and other smart speakers as we go along, as they are an important component of setting up your smarthome, but for now, let's examine using Siri (and her counterparts) as a virtual assistant with your smartphone. The idea is that you talk to her as you would another person and she helps you get things done, whether that be making a dinner reservation, finding directions, or sending a message. Siri has access to all the other built-in apps in your Apple device — think Contacts, Mail, Calendar, Maps, Safari, and so on, and can use the apps to answer questions or execute your commands. More recently Siri moved to Mac, making virtual voice assistance available on Apple laptops as well.

Siri is part of the Apple family and as such has some drawbacks. Siri is not as sophisticated as other virtual assistants such as Amazon's Alexa and Google Assistant. Apple, Amazon, and Google are the three main tech giants competing for your smarthome dollar (and data). These three giants are also fighting for primacy in the smart car as well. Of these three, Apple has the highest level of privacy protection, which is good news if the privacy of your data is your main concern, but not such good news when it comes to machine learning. Remember in Chapter 3 when we talked about data as the backbone of machine learning and artificial intelligence? Don Lekei, the in-home tech expert you met in Chapter 2, had this to say: "Both Amazon and Google collect far more data which feeds their assistants, which means both Google Assistant and Amazon's Alexa are more robust, smarter, and in many ways more effective." This is worth considering as you make decisions about your device choices. We'll revisit this later, but in the meantime, think of Siri as the "not-quite-as-smart" assistant.

2.2 Hey, Google

As noted above, virtual assistance apps aren't limited to the Apple world. For Android users, Google Assistant is the popular choice, characterized by the wake-word phrase, "Hey, Google." Originally designed as Google Now, an alternative to Apple's Siri, the renamed Google Assistant offers voice searching and commands, and voice-activated device control. Like Apple's Siri, Google Assistant can —

- access information from your calendars and contacts;
- find information online from directions and maps, to restaurants, weather, and news;
- answer simple web searches such as, "Who starred in *The Princess Bride*"?;
- control your music libraries and play video content on your Chromecast or other compatible devices;
- run timers and reminders;
- make appointments and send messages;

- open apps on your phone;

- read notifications to you;

- offer real-time spoken translations; and

- control your devices and your smarthome.

As an example, Google Assistant is the VA system built into Google Home (or Nest; more on Google branding later), Google's brand of smart speakers. From it you can essentially run your smarthome, eliminating the need to use your smartphone as a hub at all. Some may feel that having to pull out and tap, or even voice activate a phone is unnecessarily time-consuming, and a hassle, when you can simply speak into the air and have a smart speaker follow your instructions. Smartphone use is pervasive, though, and most smartphone users aren't far from their phones at any time. For those who have privacy concerns and are leery of an always-listening smart speaker, the phone as a hub is an excellent choice. The installation of apps on the smartphone is central to setting up your system anyway, and the phone also has the advantage of offering geofencing features and remote access so that you can control your devices even when you are far from home.

For one of my young journalist colleagues, using a Google Home smart speaker has become second nature. The smart speaker helps her manage her music library, set timers for recipes, and research the many subjects in which she is interested. "It's gotten to the point," she says, "where when I am walking around my neighborhood and think of something I need to do or want to know, I start saying 'Hey, Google' out loud." She laughs as she relays this anecdote, but she is part of a growing trend.

You may remember, in the early days of cell phones, how strange it seemed to see people talking on their phones in public spaces. Telephone conversations had come out of the phone booth, so to speak. More recently, as earbuds and microphones have gotten smaller it is not uncommon for it to appear as though people are walking down the street talking to themselves, when in fact they are on their smartphones. With VAs such as Siri and Google Assistant embedded in phones, watches, tablets, and the growing diversity of things in the Internet of Things, this kind of experience is becoming commonplace.

In the past, the two operating systems (iOS and Android) for Siri and Google Assistant were quite separate. Today, Apple users can download and use the Google Assistant on the iPhone and access most of the features. An excellent 2019 tutorial on installing the Google Assistant on iPhone can be found at www.lifewire.com/google-assistant-on-iphone-4628298 (accessed December 2019).

One significant issue with Google Assistant: If you have a G-Suite account with Google — the suite of web applications for businesses — you will encounter restrictions on access to the full set of Google Assistant features required to effectively use Google Home. This restriction may vary from country to country. Despite its wide availability, Google Assistant has been limited to personal Google accounts. Google is working on this. In mid-2019, Google announced an integration with G-Suite, to enable access but as a G-Suite subscriber, my experience using the Google Assistant with my Google Home Mini in Canada has been challenging.

2.3 Hello, Alexa

We've segued from exploring the role of the smartphone as the smart hub into introducing their built-in VAs — the same VAs that are built into smart speakers. Smartphones and smart speakers work in tandem. The VA discussion would not be complete without introducing you to Alexa, the VA integrated into the Amazon suite of smart devices. When Amazon developed and launched the Amazon Fire, its version of a smartphone in 2014, it was widely considered a tech disaster and was pulled from the market a year after launch. There are hints that Amazon is considering launching another phone product and may well have done so by the time this book is printed. The primary driver to enter the marketplace is to provide a smartphone home to Alexa, Amazon's powerful VA that is built into the very popular Amazon Echo and Amazon Echo Dot smart speakers. Let's meet Alexa now, and then take a look at the role of smart speakers in the connected home.

In the survey I conducted as part of the research for this book, I asked my peers if they used smart speaker services and if so, how. My friend Faye Luxemburg-Hyam, a skilled maker of artisanal beaded jewelry, had this to say: "We have Alexa built in to our Sonos speaker system and ask for countless pieces of information throughout the day — weather reports here at home and elsewhere, news highlights, election results, music requests, questions about authors and what they have written and when. I also have Alexa read my emails and messages to me, and to send texts. Alexa helps me with recipes, household and gardening advice, and where to purchase things locally. We program in reminders for appointments and things like making calls to wish people a happy birthday." For Faye and her husband Nathan, Alexa is part of their day-to-day life, providing a rich source of useful information and acting as a kind of personal secretary.

Like Google Assistant, Alexa controls a multitude of functions and is compatible with many devices.

I've focused on voice assistants here because as you look at setting up your connected home, you will likely be considering which brand of smart speaker you want to act as a hub for your ecosystem. Before we get into a discussion of the three major brands that are dominating the connected home marketplace, let me give you a little bit more information as I promised in Chapter 2, about hubs and how they function.

3. A Note about Hubs

The word "hub" is used to describe many things in the world of technology, from cloud-based data information controllers to the geographic areas in cities where physical tech businesses cluster. For our purposes, we are referring to hubs both as the devices that act as bridges that allow products from different manufacturers to communicate using different protocols or standards, and the devices that centralize and control tasks and functions via apps. As we've described in this chapter, your smartphone acts as a kind of a hub coordinating the apps needed to run your smart devices. Smart Speakers such as Amazon's Echo series with Alexa, Apple HomePod with Siri, or Google Home with Google Assistant can also function as hubs, centralizing information and functions and carrying out tasks across platforms. Still, in order to translate the different languages used by standards such as ZigBee, Z-Wave, Bluetooth, and Wi-Fi a separate physical hub or bridge may be needed. These act as switches that trigger other devices that run on different standards. Depending on your personal preferences and the scope of your connected home, you may or may not need additional hubs or bridges beyond your smartphone or smart speakers.

We will be spending quite a bit of time talking about the three main brands listed earlier and how they can function as an ecosystem in your smarthome. There are other hubs available in the marketplace that you may want to consider as well. These can integrate with the three brands mentioned here, and also function in a way as agnostic hubs, able to work with a wide variety of platforms. I will continue to emphasize that devices from a single manufacturer are more likely to work seamlessly together than a variety of devices from different manufacturers. As well these brands are trusted and tested, and more likely to address security concerns. Again, much will depend on your personal preference and aptitude for DIY networking and troubleshooting. So, let's talk about choosing the ecosystem that will best serve your needs.

4. The Connected Home Ecosystem

Clayton Brown is a product expert at one of Canada's leading consumer electronics and cell phone retail chains. His advice for those who are considering a connected home is simply to start somewhere. "You've got to get started," he said. "You'd be amazed how one thing will lead to another as you begin to install devices in your home."

Brown recommends that consumers first consider their personal preferences in regard to the various providers. For example, if you already have an Amazon Prime account, and are buying products and downloading entertainment, it might make sense for you to equip your smarthome with an Amazon Echo product's voice assistant (Alexa), an Echo Show smart display screen, an Echo Dot smart speaker, and an Amazon Fire TV streaming media stick. These devices will work pretty seamlessly together, and you will be supporting your favorite provider. You can add Alexa-compatible home products such as smart lights, locks, blinds, thermostats, and many others as you go.

Brown personally prefers the Google Home network. Google is the world's leading search engine and one of the top five technology companies worldwide, alongside Amazon, Apple, Microsoft, and Facebook. Google is compatible with both Android and iOS operating systems, as we described earlier, which can make it easy to set up and manage your systems. Samsung SmartThings and the IFTTT (If This Then That) platform are also significant players in the consumer marketplace.

My dear friend and colleague Rebecca Coleman, a respected west coast food blogger and a postsecondary social media and digital marketing instructor, is also a fan of the Google Home platform. Coleman talked about this on her blog, Cooking by Laptop, in a November 2019 post about using Google in the kitchen. "I did a bunch of research, Google Home versus Amazon's Alexa. I chose the Google Home for a few reasons: first off, I'm not a huge Amazon shopper. I don't have Prime, it's not my go-to for shopping like many people. On the other hand, I'm pretty entrenched in the Google universe — I use Gmail primarily, I have Google Drive, and it just felt like a better fit for me. The other thing I didn't like about Amazon's Alexa is that it gets triggered by saying the word Alexa So, if you're having a casual conversation and drop the word Alea it turns on. With the Google home, you have to say, 'Hey Google' or 'OK Google' to trigger it, and I find that works better." ("Using My Google Home in the Kitchen," CookingByLaptop.com, accessed December 2019.)

Coleman raises some excellent points here. Each of the three majors are different and your decision will be based partly on how you feel about them personally. As I noted earlier, I found Google Home a challenge because of the restrictions I encountered using Google Assistant with my G-Suite corporate account, which happens to be the account that governs my calendars and contacts features. Google Home also seems to be finicky, needing two apps (the Google Home app and the Google Assistant app) to function. As an Amazon shopper with an Amazon Prime account, I personally found setting up and using the Amazon Alexa assistant intuitive and easy.

Allen LaRose is a financial investment advisor and self-proclaimed tech geek. Known affectionately by his family as Gadget-man, he takes a more agnostic view. In the early days, LaRose started as a Microsoft devotee who later moved on to Apple products. His first foray into smarthome devices was with Apple TV, although he now happily runs both Google Home and Alexa smart speakers as part of his connected home network. When LaRose first decided to set up his smarthome, Apple HomePod wasn't yet on the market. As an early adapter to new technology and as someone who has a good grasp of the fundamentals, LaRose doesn't hesitate to mix and match ecosystems and tinker with his own network. He currently runs somewhere around 75 devices on his network. Says LaRose, "I prefer not to be locked into an ecosystem, gravitating toward apps that will run across platforms. I like the freedom and knowing I can switch back and forth based on features and performance."

5. The Majors: Amazon, Apple, and Google

It is important to think of smart speakers not so much as a device but rather as part of an overall ecosystem that will be used to connect and automate your smarthome devices. While the smart speaker in and of itself is a device, it is also home to the software that runs the assistants themselves. In this section let's compare the advantages of choosing one system over another. There are differences in regard to how the three main platforms perform, but by and large their functionality is basically similar. They all —

- operate as good quality audio speakers, in addition to being smart;

- include voice activated virtual assistants triggered by a wake word (Hey Google, Alexa, Hey Siri) ;

- use companion smartphone apps to function;

- can control automation of compatible smarthome devices such thermostats, lights, locks, security cameras, doorbells, and other technologies;

- can check weather, manage calendars, set timers and alarms, search the Internet, access music and other audio libraries, and send, receive, and relay some form of messages and phone calls; and

- are becoming integrated with smart car technology.

So, what are some of the aspects to consider in differentiating between the brands?

5.1 Google Assistant versus Amazon's Alexa and Apple's Siri

Google is by far and away the favorite for Android users, and also has the most expertise when it comes to search. It is Google, after all! Google Assistant, the app that runs with Google Home and the suite of connected Nest products, is the same across all of your devices so as long as you're logged in to your account, it will remember your preferences. Many users also find the Google Home set up to be easy. From the Google Home app, you can set up, manage, and control your Google Chromecast video-streaming devices plus hundreds of connected home products. Google's main strength lies in the robust search function and accuracy of information. As Google has rebranded products there is some confusion for consumers in regard to terms like Google Home and Google Nest, but this is likely to resolve itself over time.

Alexa, the software found in the Amazon Echo line of smart speakers (as well as in Sonos, Fitbit, and many other products) offers you a wider range of things you can do than Google does. In addition to its native applications, Alexa has a long list of functions, referred to as "skills" that can be accessed through the app. As of April 2019, there are more than 90,000 skills available for users to download on their Alexa-enabled devices. Depending on where you live, you may also be able to manage and control your Amazon Fire TV via Alexa. You cannot control Chromecast via Alexa nor can you control Fire TV via Google. Neither is compatible with Apple TV. As an Amazon platform, Alexa's main strength lies in understanding and tracking our personal habits and preferences.

Both Google and Amazon have worked hard with partners to create compatibility with third-party devices and both brands have also developed lower cost devices — Echo Dot and Google Mini for example — that work pretty much exactly like their more expensive siblings, which means you can affordably add devices to all areas of your home. Unlike Apple, both of these brands also recently launched smart displays (Google Nest Hub and Google Hub Max and the Echo Tap, Echo Show, and Echo Spot) that are compatible with their systems. Display screens are very useful for things such as recipes, song lists, search results, video calling, and weather. As facial recognition technology becomes more commonplace, video interface with these kinds of devices is likely not far behind. If you like to be a little ahead of the curve, this is worth thinking about.

Apple's Siri was the last one out of the gate in terms of having a smart speaker home even though it was the first smartphone voice assistant on the market. As we noted earlier Siri has more limits than the other two, in terms of adaptive learning and in terms of skills and actions. Remember that these limitations result from the fact that the Apple system has more robust privacy and data collection policies —worth considering if that is important to you. Experts agree that the Apple HomePod offers the best speaker, both for multidirectional voice activation and audio quality playback sound. Sonos (with Alexa built in) runs a close second. This, and compatibility with Apple Music, is Apple's main strength. The speaker has spatial awareness and automatically analyzes the acoustics and adjusts the sound based on its location. When you add HomePods to multiple rooms, the speakers communicate with each other through AirPlay.

Through Apple HomePod, Siri controls Apple's HomeKit platform of connected devices, including Apple TV. HomeKit is a software framework whereby users set up their iOS device to configure, communicate with, and control smarthome appliances and devices. Through the HomeKit service, users can enable automatic actions in the house either through a simple voice dictation to Siri via speaker or smartphone or through apps. If you are an iPhone user or in the Apple camp in regard to personal preference, setting up your connected home with native Apple products will make sense. Apple got a later start in the market and is a more proprietary brand than either Google or Amazon, so you may find there are fewer official Apple-compatible devices available at this time.

5.2 The social side of smart speakers: family, friends, and visitors

The three brands also differ in how they approach the very real privacy concerns commensurate with having an "always listening" device in your home, potentially eavesdropping on you and your guests. If your smart speaker is set up to send and receive your personal messages and calls, what is to prevent family members or visitors from accessing these? In general, Apple gets higher marks in the security area with a promise that HomePod won't start listening until you wake it up. Data collected is encrypted and anonymous, unlike the Google Home and Amazon Echo systems (who want to use the data for targeted advertising). HomePod also won't deliver personal notifications if the primary user is not at home. Google Home does not record your conversations other than to send them to the system to fulfill whatever request you have made. People in your home can request personal information and activate your device. With Google Home you can schedule downtime to turn off the device, or turn it off manually. With Alexa, at the time of this writing, you can manually mute the

Echos, and you can instruct Alexa to delete your daily recordings via voice command, or within the settings feature. You can also schedule recordings to be deleted automatically. All three have multiple voice recognition so you can set up voice profiles and personalize them for family members, but this does not guarantee privacy.

Visitors or guests in your home may be uncomfortable with these devices. My best advice is to let your guests know you have them and to simply turn them off to ensure privacy. In the event that you want to share the functionality and control of the devices with visitors, settings can be adjusted for guest modes that enable temporary access.

What about the children or grandchildren in your home? In her book, *Digital Life Skills for Youth* (Self-Counsel Press, 2019), Angela Crocker puts it plainly, "Youth need to know how to operate [the Internet of Things] for their safety and the comfort of their family." I asked Crocker to comment further on this subject. Here is what she had to say:

"The Internet of Things adds a new and complicated layer of digital skills to teach children and youth. If a family decides to bring the IoT into their home, family members of all ages will, to some extent, interact with those devices. But, it's important to consider the developmental readiness of younger digital citizens. If you teach a preschooler to use a smart speaker to play music or instruct a virtual assistant to turn on the lights, is that the right skill for their developmental age and stage? As the IoT is not, yet, found everywhere, shouldn't that child also learn the analog way to do things? Of course, as children get older they must develop digital skills. My work focuses on the tween and teen years — the journey from childhood to adulthood — when most youth are ready to learn digital skills. While the exact age will vary, most youth have the maturity to understand the security implications and self-regulation to know when it's socially acceptable to engage IoT devices. And it's important to remember that youth need guidance to develop the digital skills to understand security, privacy, and more in the context of the IoT."

Life in the modern smarthome is still family life, and the ages, stages, and tech readiness of individual members of the family need to be part of the decision-making process. From toddlers to elders, technology can serve all.

A recent study in the United Kingdom found that nearly half a million older people go as much as five days a week without speaking to anyone. Social isolation has been linked to depression and related health and quality of life issues. According to the Voice For Loneliness study, speaking on a regular basis with a voice assistant can help boost the mood and emotional health of people who have restricted social contact due to age and associated mobility issues (www.greenwoodcampbell.com/what/voiceforloneliness, accessed December 2019).

6. Final Words of Advice on Choosing a Smart Device Ecosystem

Smart products are evolving at a rapid rate and much may have changed by the time you read this. It is also worth keeping in mind that there are many, many, devices and "things" in the Internet of Things world that are not manufactured by nor compatible with the three major brands we have described here. What we are focusing on in this section is a decision between ecosystems, not devices.

Many of the technology experts I interviewed for the book agreed with Clayton Brown and recommended that consumers set up the initial connected home system with one of the three major technology providers — the Amazon, Google, or Apple ecosystems. Yes, this will make you beholden to continuing to use their devices and there is a risk that some of the products will become obsolete (which will likely happen over time anyway), but for the non-techy, this is sound advice.

Remember, you need not include a smart speaker or voice-activated virtual assistant as part of your ecosystem if you are concerned about privacy or additional complexity. Your connected home (and other aspects of your smart life) can be managed through smartphone apps without using a smart speaker. If you do decide to use one (or more) of the three majors, all offer detailed installation and user guides that are full of useful tips and are available online.

At the time of this writing, both *The Simple Amazon Alexa User Guide* by Clayton M. Rines (independently published, 2019), and *Google Home: Ultimate Guide to Quickstart Your Google Home Experience* by Kyle Black (CreateSpace, 2017) were available to download free of charge from Amazon through my Kindle Unlimited account and *Apple HomePod: Master your HomePod User Guide and Manual* by Roman Alexander (independently published, 2018) was less than $10 CAD to purchase and download. There are also downloadable guides available for specific generations of devices. New and updated guides will continue to be published, so be sure to check publication dates.

Another option is to enlist professionals and hire a tech service provider to take care of installation and maintenance for you. Home automation is not really new and there are many companies that are offering both large- and small-scale smarthome installation and home automation. For larger smarthome investments, such as appliances, gas or electric fireplaces, security systems, or window coverings, in-home installation is often included with the purchase or for a small fee. As with other decisions related to in-home IoT, look for compatibility in regard to product specifications and understand the terms of service. Do your research and consider your preferences. Talk to friends and family who may be using these products. Visit your local retailers and talk to their staff.

5
Smart Goods and Gadgets for Your Connected Home

Do you remember the animated sitcom *The Jetsons*? It was produced by Hanna-Barbera in the United States in the 1960s and then again in the 1980s. The weekly cartoon took an entertaining and futuristic look at the daily lives of George and Jane Jetson and their two children, Judy and Elroy, a dog named Astro, and a robot named Rosie. George commutes via aerocar and works very few hours a week. In the stereotype of the times, Jane is a homemaker. Their life is portrayed as leisurely, aided by numerous time and labor-saving devices and technological conveniences. Nevertheless, these conveniences occasionally break down, usually triggering humorous consequences. Despite the purported simplicity and ease of future domestic life, *The Jetsons* regularly encounter stress and see themselves as overworked. In some episodes, the conveniences they enjoy seem to not be worth the trouble they cause. The Jetsons proved to be surprisingly accurate in much of the gadgetry they portrayed, including microwave ovens, video calling, and smartwatches. The show also effectively captured the somewhat ambiguous relationship between humans and time-saving technology.

To automate or not to automate? How smart do you want your smarthome to be? Is installation and maintenance worth the time and trouble? In addition to apprehensions about privacy and security, these are the questions you need to think about as you examine the many goods and gadgets now available with embedded smart technology. You need to understand what my friend and technology expert, Steve Dotto, calls the *quid pro quo* of technology use "the trade-off between convenience and privacy." In a simple analogy, Dotto offers this: "Back in the day, if you hired a housekeeper, you knew you would be giving up some personal privacy. It was a risk you were willing to take for the convenience and benefit of having someone else clean your house."

As well as understanding this trade-off, it is important to assess your own tolerance and aptitude for learning new things and adapting or troubleshooting as things change. Some areas of adaptation to smart technology are easier than others, simply because we are more used to the products. Security cameras and motion-activated lights, for example, have been in the marketplace for some time. Baby monitors, pet-tracking devices, and automated blinds and window coverings are fairly commonplace. Smarthome technology is now available for virtually every area of your home. Their purpose is ultimately to make our homes more convenient, safer, and more energy efficient. Only you can decide which devices and systems are right for you. Let's run through some of the common household smart goods.

1. Safety and Security in Your Home

For many years, home security companies have offered remote monitoring of our homes. Motion detectors, video monitoring, night vision, automatic security lights, and other security technologies that monitor the interiors and exteriors of our homes provide safeguards against intrusion. Today, consumers can choose to install and monitor private home security systems that can be controlled via smartphone apps and smart-speaker hubs. Many systems also offer third-party monitoring, usually for a monthly fee. The scope, scale, and costs vary depending on the service provider. Smart cameras, smart locks, and smart doorbells can also integrate with your security system. There are many types of smart door locks and smart doorbells. Most are battery powered, however some may require a power source, so wiring may be required.

A great example of this technology is the Ring video doorbell. Ring is a smart doorbell that includes a high-definition camera, a motion sensor, and a microphone and speaker for two-way audio communication, integrated with an associated mobile app. Users can view real-time video from the camera, receive notifications when someone rings the doorbell, and communicate with visitors through the integrated speaker and microphone. It also operates as a surveillance camera and automatically triggers recordings when rung or when motion sensors are activated. Ring is compatible with Alexa, Google Home, and Apple HomeKit. According to SafeWise, an independent review site, the following are the ten best wireless security cameras of 2019:

- Arlo Pro

- Wyze Cam Pan

- Canary All-in-One Home Security Device

- Ring Spotlight Cam

- Reolink Argus 2

- Amcrest ProHD Indoor

- Amazon Cloud Cam

- Google Nest Cam Indoor

- YI Dome Camera

- Adobe Iota

You can read more about their specific features and compatibility here: www.safewise.com/blog/best-wireless-security-cameras.

2. People and Pets: Protecting the Ones We Love

Smart technologies, complete with internet-connected audio and video-monitoring devices, raise significant concerns about the potential for strangers to violate our privacy by hacking these devices and spying on your family at home. At the same time, these devices enable us to keep a closer watch on our young children, vulnerable elders, and pets.

The home baby monitor — first introduced with radio transmitter audio technology in the 1930s — has evolved to the point where we can not only see and hear our children, but we can measure their breathing and temperature, even from a remote location, via mobile phone. This may be useful both in the moment and in aggregating a picture of a child's health over weeks and months. At the high end of the market, you can instruct your monitoring device to play selected lullabies or rock your baby's specially designed bed.

For some, the need for this monitoring complexity may be open to question. Adrienne So, in a *Wired* magazine survey of available baby monitors, points out that a healthy baby's cries are generally loud enough to more than rouse the adults in a normal-sized home. Her all-around pick for best baby monitor is the Eufy Spaceview, which operates on radio frequencies without any Wi-Fi or internet connection. This device, operated from a mobile phone from within the home, delivers audio and video signals and can perform a 360-degree scan of the baby's room. An even simpler solution is to set up a mobile phone as a camera in the baby's room, with the signal sent to a second phone. Both of these options will protect the system from outside intrusion. ("The 8 Best Baby Monitors to Keep you Sane at Night," Wired.com, accessed December 2019.)

If you have an autistic child who wanders, or an adult with dementia or another cognitive disorder, you have probably checked out the available range of location devices. Alzheimers.net puts the AngelSense locator at the top of its list. This system includes a GPS tracker device that locks onto the wearer's clothing. Using geofencing features, it can be programmed to send an alarm when the wearer moves outside of a designated safe area or fails to arrive at a designated safe location on time, and it offers two-way voice communication. Parents or caregivers can forward the location of the GPS tracker to family or emergency responders. The iTraq locator, with some of the same features, also reports on the ambient temperature at the wearer's location. This is the enabling technology that also allows the system to respond to individual preferences in the smarthome, automatically changing the scene or set of routines as the wearer enters or leaves a room. We'll talk more about routines and scenes in section 7.

The principles behind the personal locator have also been applied to pet locators. A 2019 product review in Pet Life Today selected the Whistle 3 GPS Pet Tracker and Activity Monitor as the best on the market. This GPS tracker sends an email or text when your dog leaves a designated safe area. The Whistle 3 also acts as a fitness and health monitor, measuring the dog's activity levels along with the amount of time the dog devotes to self-licking, scratching, and sleeping. Dog owners can collect the reports based on this data and submit them to their veterinarians at regular intervals. As a rule, the GPS systems for both people and pets are subject to a monthly subscription fee. ("The Best GPS Dog Trackers and Collars 2019," PetLifeToday.com, accessed December 2019.)

Another popular pet related device is the Furbo Dog Camera. Furbo is an interactive pet camera and integrated app that enables you to see, talk, and even robotically toss treats to your dog when you're not home. The same company produces the Furbo Dog Nanny that gives dog owners additional features including 24/7 alerts that provide activity, barking, person, and selfie alerts, along with cloud-recorded videos triggered by the same activities. A rather sweet feature is Doggie Diaries, a 90-second time lapse of highlights from your dog's day.

3. Home Maintenance

There are other smart devices you may wish to consider to enhance your family's safety and the security of your home. In addition to the cameras, doorbells, door locks, and wearable tracking and security devices discussed earlier, you may want to consider smarthome smoke detectors or gas or water leak detectors as well. These devices come as DIY options, or you can choose to have them installed as part of your whole home connected system. There are also automated smarthome watering and irrigation systems for your lawn and garden; garden monitors that collect and analyze data on light, soil, and moisture conditions; and smart robotic lawnmowers.

4. A More Comfortable Home: Lighting, Window Coverings, and Temperature Control

4.1 Lighting

Lighting is one of the most important investments you make in your home. It is what sets the mood or tone in any given room and is also responsible for a large amount of energy consumption and associated costs. You want home lighting to be aesthetically pleasing but also environmentally responsible and economical.

If you have your lighting professionally installed by a contractor, they will be able to advise you on smart lighting options. Individual consumers will find the staff at local specialty lighting stores very knowledgeable. Nearly all big box retail hardware stores carry a range of smart lighting options including bulbs, plugs, switches, panels, and light strips.

Let's not neglect the outdoors. Smart path lights, spotlights, security lights, and even twinkle lights are available for your yard, garden, or patio. New technology is fundamentally changing the way we use lighting to decorate at home. Easy-to-install interlocking LED panels, light strips, and color-tunable bulbs all offer new options for using light to create moods and scenes and enhance decor.

Today, most consumers choose LED lightbulbs as they consume less energy than incandescent bulbs and last considerably longer. Initially, they are more costly to buy than incandescent bulbs (although prices are coming down); however, the cost is offset by the longevity of the product. Because of their long lifespan they are ideal for use in hard to reach places such as ceiling fixtures and pot lights. LED smart bulbs can be turned off and on, change color, or be dimmed remotely from your smartphone.

In Chapter 2 we talked about the different network systems that support your connected home. Before you decide on what kind of smart bulbs, plugs, or switches to invest in, be sure to determine what technology is right for you. At the time of this writing, Philips Hue bulbs are leading the market. The Philips Hue ecosystem is the most comprehensive and uses the ZigBee protocol. The starter kit comes with a ZigBee hub (remember, this is the bridge needed so the devices can communicate with Wi-Fi and each other). Philips recently added a Bluetooth version of Hue bulbs to its lineup and many other manufacturers make Bluetooth bulbs that skip the home network altogether. These can be easy to set up and manage although they can't be controlled from outside the home.

There are also bulbs and plugs that communicate directly with Wi-Fi, and no hub or bridge is required. Typically, these are less expensive than the Hue line, and relatively easy to manage from your phone or smart speaker. Wi-Fi connected bulbs, switches, or plugs will also work best if you want to coordinate them with a broader smarthome system. Bluetooth bulbs can pair with your smartphone but can't connect with other sensors and so on in your home. Another issue is that wired-in dimmers or other features may not work with smart bulbs, although some of the smart bulbs or strips themselves can be dimmed. Before you buy it is important to check the product specifications in regard to compatibility with your system, including whether they can be controlled by voice command via Alexa, Google Home, or Siri, if you are using a virtual assistant as a hub.

4.2 Window coverings

Similar to smart lighting, with automatic or smart blinds and draperies there are professionals who can help you design, choose, and install the right combination for your home. DIY options are also available online and from local retailers. Smart blinds work via technology called wireless motorization. They can be controlled with your smartphone, tablet, or by a specific controller, similar to a television remote. Depending on the manufacturer, they can be integrated with voice control using Alexa, Siri, or Google Assistant. Some have a native voice control built in.

Using the related apps you can set up and schedule room scenes that meet your specific light and privacy needs throughout the day. Many products can be programmed to open at sunrise and close at sunset based on your specific geographic location. By carefully checking the product specifications you will be able to determine what automatic blinds or drapery motorization is right for you.

4.3 The smart thermostat: Too hot, too cold, or just right?

Many of us are probably familiar with some version of automatic thermostats, preprogramming them to come on in the morning and turn off at night or raise and lower the temperature based on the family's specific daily schedule.

Thermostats typically control heating, cooling, and ventilation in your home. Heating a home when it is empty is not only costly, it also wastes precious energy resources. These are the considerations that motivated many to invest in early versions of programmable thermostats. Essentially, all you needed to do was select your heating and cooling options and set and schedule the desired temperatures and the thermostat did the rest.

Today's smart thermostats go beyond simple temperature detection and adjustment allowing you to adjust your home's temperature remotely and integrate thermostat settings with preprogrammed schedules or what are called scenes or routines. Many, such as the Nest Learning Thermostat, adapt to your behavior over time, and make adjustments that will help you save energy, and be more comfortable. As always, it is important to understand how your home's specific HVAC system currently runs. While many of these products are designed to be DIY, minor rewiring may be required, especially in older homes. In any cases where electrical rewiring or adaptation is required, it is best to consult a professional.

An excellent resource for current, straightforward tech updates and information presented in a non-geeky way is the UK/US based website www.pocket-lint.com.

5. Appliances, Large and Small

A great deal of thought usually goes into selecting and choosing our large appliances such as refrigerators, ranges, washers and dryers, and dishwashers. These tend to be on the higher end of the domestic purchase scale, and we hope that these machines will last us a good number of years. In terms of smart appliances, much will depend on your budget. The more you are willing to invest, the more features that will come included in your appliance bundle. When we are looking at purchasing large appliances, the size, dimension, and design of the appliance matters, as well as its capacity. In my opinion, the first thing to consider is your family's needs. Then, once you have established what it is you need in a large appliance, consider your budget. How much are you willing to spend? Most smart appliances will include the following features:

- Wi-Fi connectivity to send alerts to your smartphone and integrate into your connected smarthome network.

- Compatibility with VAs such as Google Assistant, Apple's Siri, and Amazon's Alexa.

- Self-monitoring functions that spot trouble before it occurs and notify you when repairs or maintenance or needed.

- Automation features.

- Some form of energy consumption monitoring and control.

Appliances such as refrigerators that are equipped with built-in hot and cold water dispensers or coffee brewers can be programmed to come on at specific times and coordinated with the smarthome apps discussed in the previous chapter. Some smart fridges come with downloadable apps that notify your phone if the door is left open or connect to cameras that can monitor the contents of your fridge. Some include integration with food ordering services.

Similarly, smart ovens and stovetops can connect via Wi-Fi or Bluetooth to companion apps so that they can be controlled remotely or have functions set automatically. For example, you can set the oven to preheat, adjust cooking temperature, and turn off the oven from anywhere using your smartphone. Depending on the product, some connect to apps that provide recipe steps and can automatically preheat the oven to the correct temperature setting, cook food for the proper amount of time, and then turn the oven off based on recipe instructions. Stoves may also have voice activation or connect with Alexa, Google Assistant, or Siri. Smart stoves have all the same features as conventional ovens, but they may have more flexible cooktop configurations and induction burners to make cooking faster than ever.

Dishwashers, washers and dryers, and nearly every type of small home appliance is now available with smart technology. Microwave ovens, range hoods, blenders, crockpots, kitchen scales, vacuum cleaners, coffee makers, kitchen thermometers, toaster ovens and toasters, deep fryers — the list goes on. There is even a smart scanner that attaches to your kitchen garbage can that scans items as you throw them away, adding them to your smart shopping list. Nearly all of these will connect to your smarthome hub via smartphone apps or smart speakers.

6. Private Spaces: The Smart Bedroom and Bathroom

Smart technology has found its way into the bedroom and bathroom as well. Smart beds adjust to body temperature, body movement, and pressure. There are four main components to consider when thinking about investing in a smart bed:

1. **The app:** Like nearly all smart products you will need to download and install an app to control the settings on your bed. A good tip is to test out the app before you buy to be sure it is easy to use and has the features you want.

2. **A sleep tracker:** This feature monitors how long you sleep, how well, and how many times you get up in the night. Some monitor heart rate, breathing, and body temperature. Charts give you data on how well you sleep over time.

3. **Firmness and temperature adjustment:** Look for a product with dual zone control so that you and your partner can each adjust firmness and temperature to suit individual preferences.

4. **Smart support:** Does the product integrate with Amazon Alexa, Google Home/Nest, or other smart hubs? Remember, be sure to check for compatibility so you can easily and seamlessly control your connected home.

Although there is nothing quite like a good night's sleep, I personally prefer to avoid having too much tech in the bedroom, so I'm undecided about whether or not a smart bed would be beneficial for me.

Another consideration is cost. Good mattresses are already expensive, smart mattresses even more so. If you are going to invest in one, make sure it has the features you need and that it can integrate with the rest of your system. If a smart bed is beyond the budget, there are many sleep-tracking apps in the marketplace. As with most choices in the connected home, budget, efficiency, and personal preference play key roles in decision-making.

6.1 Mirror, mirror on the wall: The smart bathroom

A very useful feature for the smart bathroom is the smart mirror. A smart mirror is a two-way mirror with an electronic display behind the glass. The display shows the user different kinds of information such as weather, time, date, and news updates. Displays can be customized and can even include your calendar, social media feeds, and work with voice assistants such as Alexa. Yes, you can ask your mirror questions!

You can also set reminders or control other smart devices in your home. There are mirrors that double as smart screens. Some have screen casting capabilities, video calling capabilities, or sensor controls where they can recognize you when you enter the bathroom. Basic smart mirrors are available in easy-to-install kits or can be installed by a professional.

Other smart bathroom gadgets include Bluetooth connected in-shower speakers; motion- or voice-activated mirror lights or other lighting; and Wi-Fi enabled smart scales that document your accurate weight, record Body Mass Index (BMI), body fat measurements, and your heart rate. Some scales feature automatic user recognition and connect to Fitbits or Apple Watches.

6.2 The smart toilet

I first encountered the Japanese smart toilet seat while staying at a rather lovely hotel run by a Japanese consortium. The toilet seat offered a mystifying array of choices including seat angle, temperature, music and sound, and a selection of wand-washing sprays depending on the nature of your "business." In addition to this variety of features, the toilet seat sort of revved up when you sat down making a kind of purring or humming noise on contact. I found this rather disconcerting, particularly in the middle of the night. As I had a hard time deciphering the symbology and language on the device, I opted to simply pull out the plug disconnecting it from the power source.

I understood the intent of the device, but it wasn't really meeting a need I felt I had to fill. I may simply be too old-fashioned for this particular tech. There is potential, though, for smart toilets to do much more than make our toilet time more comfortable, more sanitary, and less embarrassing.

Sameer Berry, a gastroenterologist-in-training at Cedars-Sinai Medical Center in Los Angeles, said in an article for CNBC.com, "Lots of companies have tried to create a health-tracking toilet, but most have failed to deliver on their goals because they offer gimmicky monitoring or lack evidence that their data can accurately track health outcomes. Toilet manufacturing giants Toto and Matsushita made a step in the right direction when they released Wi-Fi-connected toilets that measure body mass index, biochemical makeup (sugar, protein), flow rate, and temperature of urine. Inui Health (formerly known as Scanadu) announced FDA approval for its smartphone-connected urine analysis which can detect bladder infections, pre- and gestational diabetes, and kidney disease, all in the comfort of one's home."

Taking this a step further, if the data collected by your smart toilet can offer detailed diagnostic information, it can certainly help shape shopping and diet choices. Why not have the health data analysis sent from your toilet to an app that can recommend the right foods and recipes to improve your health profile? The app could connect directly to your smart fridge where the technology can check to see if in fact you have the ingredients on hand to best support your health and well-being. If not, a shopping list automatically sent to your local food delivery service could have ingredients delivered to direct to your doorstep. Voila! From toilet to tabletop.

This is not far-fetched. We have the available technology today to create a scenario like this. It is simply a matter of getting the technology into the marketplace, using machine learning and artificial intelligence to do the analysis and having the right connected apps set up the routine.

7. Routines and Scenes

In Chapter 4 we discussed the control hubs: smartphone apps, smart speaker assistants, and other kinds of hubs or bridges used to install and manage the tasks and function assigned to your smarthome devices. With these apps you can automate what are known as scenes or routines, a preprogrammed group of automated functions that occur based on a timed schedule or are set off by triggered actions such as in the smart toilet example in section 6.2. A more typical example is one where you preset, say, a morning routine where your blinds automatically open, lights go on, the weather news is broadcast, and your coffeemaker starts brewing. Depending on your system, the applications will vary in how they are set up and in what they are called. This is another example where internet search is your friend. Go online, look up your device, and look up the possibilities for automating the functions and creating scenes or routines via either voice command or app control on the smartphone.

8. Key Principles to Guide Your Choices

By now it is clear that there are several key principles that you need to consider in bringing the Internet of Things into your daily life. They are as follows:

- Enlist the professionals. Whether you go online or visit a local retailer in person, technology experts abound, and they are very generous in sharing their time and information. If budget allows, and the scope of your connected life is comprehensive, many companies are happy to install and maintain your systems for you. I've included some of my favorite go-to resources throughout this book. Feel free to contact them. Most of them can be found easily online. There are a number of tech websites and YouTube accounts that are worth following for up-to-date information and product reviews. Also, get comfortable using the helpdesks and support chats available to you for most products and services.

- Ensure that your Wi-Fi is current and robust enough to handle your family's needs. If you read Chapter 4 and did some research, you will have a good idea of what kind of system you need to support your connected home. Remember that there are different frequencies on Wi-Fi, and that you may need a hub or a bridge so the different networks can communicate. You may need an additional router to support your home network, or you may need to upgrade your equipment.

- Make your system as secure as possible. Understand that you are trading a certain amount of privacy and a great deal of data in exchange for the use of the products and services offered by various platforms. The most important thing you can do in regard to the security of your systems is ensure that you have good, strong passwords. Read and understand the privacy policies and the settings of the devices that you choose to use.

- Always check the product specifications before you buy and go shopping either online or in person with a clear understanding of what you need. Internet search is your friend here. Look up products that you are considering purchasing. Check for compatibility with your system, and with the voice assistant you may use.

- Keep in mind that it is easier to integrate a system when all the parts all come from one manufacturer. The three main brands leading the smarthome market are Apple with their HomeKit platform and HomePod system, Google Home/Nest and the Google Assistant, and the Amazon Alexa system. Every platform has pros and cons. You may have personal preferences or favorites based on what you are using now and what you are used to, or you may prefer an agnostic system. Keep in mind that an agnostic system will require more tech savvy from you, or more help from the professionals.

- Remember, different countries, or even regions within countries, have different rules about consumer access to entertainment programming, as well as vastly inconsistent regulations and legislation governing things such as privacy and data collection. Manufacturers may offer different product lines for different markets, and software updates and new features do not necessarily roll out equally everywhere.

- Consider your actual needs. Much of the new smarthome technology is still in what I would call the novelty phase. It is fun, and interesting to play with, but does it really enhance your quality of life? Do you need a smart toaster if your dumb toaster works well enough? Perhaps you live in a very safe neighborhood or a building that offers security and maintenance as part of your homeowner fees. In that case, a smarthome security camera system and the associated technology may be of little value to you. Thinking carefully about what you actually need, consulting with family members, and basing your decisions on these reflections will save you time, money, and frustration.

Mainly, the skills you will require are patience, curiosity, and adaptability. We are in the very early days — what some are calling the wild west of the Internet of Things. Much of what is written here may have changed by the time the book is printed, and products and systems that you may be using now may become obsolete in a very short time. All of them will require some setup and maintenance or adjustment. You will want to balance the values of economy and efficiency, with your own tolerance for change and adaptation.

See Worksheet 4 before you invest in smart goods and gadgets for your home.

Worksheet 4
Applying the Key Principles: A Checklist

Before you embark on investing time and money on Internet of Things technology, use this checklist to make sure you are ready.

Checklist Questions	Yes	No
I have one or more professionals or tech-savvy contacts that can help install and troubleshoot my system.	☒	☐
My Wi-Fi and equipment have been upgraded and/or checked to ensure they are robust enough to handle my IoT needs.	☐	☒
My internet passwords are strong, and I have done my best to ensure my systems are secure.	☒	☐
I have thought through the options in regard to products and have decided to either go with a single platform (Google, Apple, or Amazon) or a more agnostic system (or some combination thereof).	☒	☐
I have researched products online and checked their system requirements and compatibility with other components of my network.	☒	☐
I understand the limits and regulations in my country, state, province, or region in regard to streaming access for entertainment.	☐	☒
I have read and understood the Terms of Service agreements related to the products I wish to use and understand the risks to privacy and security	☐	☒
I have consulted with my family or other members of my household to assess their degree of comfort with using IoT technology in the home.	☒	☐
I have evaluated the household's needs and preferences in regard to adding smart gadgets and goods or replacing older technology with new smart technology. I am confident about navigating the changes.	☒	☐

6
Connected
Home Entertainment

No discussion of the connected home would be complete without including in-home entertainment. As a result of machine learning and artificial intelligence (AI) we are now able to fully personalize our entertainment consumption. Machine learning uses algorithms to build models that help computers analyze and "learn" from data. This knowledge about our habits and preferences is stored, and our smart devices are able to make recommendations based on the data. This is much the same as the process that occurs if you search for the word pajamas in Google, and then you find behaviorally targeted advertisements for jammies popping up in your social media feeds, Messenger app, or on websites you visit. In the world of at-home entertainment, service providers such as Netflix and Spotify are able to monitor and target our viewing or listening preferences and make recommendations that are surprisingly accurate.

Consider the impacts of artificial intelligence and machine learning and the predictive models they generate on other aspects of personal entertainment such as travel, shopping, or web surfing. Via the Internet of Things and the apps we download, our devices can connect with airlines, hotel concierges, transit, restaurants, and our favorite retailers. Not only can we be notified of specials, discounts, rate adjustments, or itinerary changes and delays — all services that are already very common — we will soon be personally greeted by robot hotel concierges or store clerks and guided seamlessly to our preferred accommodation or shopping aisles. Perhaps you will prefer to eliminate the hassle of physical travel altogether, and take advantage of virtual reality, the ultimate in armchair travel? Virtual and augmented reality may offer unprecedented leisure experiences and opportunities for an aging population or for those with physical disabilities or limitations.

We are living in a time when all aspects of our lives are changing as a result of advances in technology. Many of these innovations will make our leisure pursuits more fun, more interesting, and much more personalized and self-directed. At the same time, it means we must learn new ways of doing things, ensure that our smartphones are constantly charged, and that we have the right apps downloaded in order to manage and access new technologies. We must have systems in our homes that are robust enough to handle the traffic required by Wi-Fi-enabled entertainment choices. We are in a transition period, and while it is exciting to live in a world of choice, it can be troublesome and difficult to navigate.

1. What's on TV, Besides Everything?

In terms of home entertainment, Netflix changed the game. Video streaming went mainstream, so to speak, and we could stream an amazing array of entertainment choices on our iPads, smartphones, laptops, and the multiple television flat screens throughout our homes. Movie libraries on CDs and videotapes quickly became obsolete. As a result, a new consumer entertainment standard is emerging called OTT (for "over the top"). The term is commonly applied to media services such as video-on-demand platforms, but can refer to messaging services, audio steaming, internet-based calling services, or any online content provider that offers media streaming as a standalone product. Typically, these are subscription services that don't rely on traditional media distribution channels such as telecommunications networks or cable television providers. All you need is access to an internet connection and you can get into your services at any time. There are now many subscription-streaming channels in the marketplace, including streaming apps for most traditional television networks as well. Even the most basic smart TVs come equipped with Netflix and YouTube apps as native features.

Music-streaming services such as Spotify have revolutionized the way we buy, sort, find, store, and broadcast music and radio choices. Most of our media choices can also be controlled and managed through our smarthome hubs and the apps that control them. This technology is emerging, and perfect synchronicity is not yet achieved, but it is not far behind. One of the best aspects of streaming technology is that it is relatively simple to use, primarily requiring a simple log-in and password. The lists that follow itemize some of the more common music- and video-streaming services.

Music streaming platforms at time of writing include:

- Amazon Music

- Apple Music

- Google Play Music

- iHeart Radio

- Pandora

- SiriusXM

- SoundCloud

- Spotify

- Xbox Music

Some of most common household video-streaming platforms at the time of writing include:

- Amazon Prime

- Crave

- Disney+

- Facebook Watch

- Fubo TV

- Gem

- HBO

- Hulu

- Netflix

- Sling TV

- Vimeo

- YouTube

Any or all of these platforms (and many other specialized streaming services) can be available via your smart TV. It is important to note, however, that all smart TVs are not equal. According to an article by Alexis Madrigal in *The Atlantic*, "Analysts estimate that smart TVs now make up about 70 percent of all new TV sales. The television is no longer a mere display, but a full-fledged computer, for good and for ill. " ("Your TV Is Now a Computer, but Not in a Good Way," The Atlantic.com, January 24, 2019.)

A new television set used to represent a fairly significant family purchase, but smart TVs are now relatively inexpensive to buy. In the same Atlantic article, Madrigal had this to say: " ... after you've purchased an internet-connected device of any kind, it begins to generate information that the company can use itself or sell to third parties." Madrigal references commentary from Bill Baxter, chief technology officer of Vizio, a major television manufacturer. Baxter told "The Verge" that the reason his company can sell TVs so cheaply now is that it makes up the money by selling bits of data and access to your TV after you purchase it. Baxter called this "post-purchase monetization."

In much the same way that other connected devices gather and use our personal data, the right of television manufacturers to sell access to our televisions to third parties can usually be found in the fine print of the Terms of Service agreement. Most of us don't really pay that much attention to these agreements.

The television as computer creates all kinds of complexities as well as potential problems for typical users — particularly those who are not overly tech savvy. In making decisions about what kind of smart TV to invest in, or in making decisions about streaming services, first consider your own entertainment viewing preferences.

During a recent household move, my husband and I had the opportunity to reconsider our choices. The move required us to disconnect our existing services and decide which services and options we wanted to reconnect in our new home. One of our considerations was whether to "cut the cord" from our cable television provider.

In October of 2019, I conducted an anecdotal online poll of friends and peers. I asked them if and when they had cut the cable cord and what they were using instead. Most who had cut the cord started doing so as early as 2013, replacing their cable boxes with streaming services such as Netflix, Crave, Roku, Apple TV, or Amazon Prime, to name a few.

Rebecca Vaughn, a colleague who is a writer and a communications manager for a local city government, has put a lot of thought into her choices. In addition to being a tech-savvy professional, Vaughn is an avid sports fan and a single mom. Says Vaughn, "I have a Samsung Smart TV. I have a Netflix app, Amazon Prime app, and a DAZN sports app on it that I have purchased subscriptions to. All three subscriptions together come to around $35 CAD a month, which is far better than the $150/month for basic cable and then having to pay for add-on packages I'd need to get the other channels I want. All three subscriptions let me watch on several devices and there is nothing I feel I'm missing out on. My sports app gives me the all the NFL games including the Super Bowl (and my dad can use it to watch Premier League). I get my news from news outlets via social media and my CBC Radio app on my phone, which I listen to in the morning. I have all the shows I could possibly want on Amazon Prime (plus Amazon shipping benefits!) and Netflix, which has great TV shows and movies. (I find when I watch regular cable, I think the shows are cheesy; I mean there's plenty of trash TV on Netflix, but regular cable shows like *The Masked Singer*? Not my bag!) I would like to get Google Chromecast so I can voice control my TV but haven't looked into it yet."

What I love about this example is that Vaughn is very neatly illustrating the way we can completely personalize individual viewing experiences. Not only are Vaughn and her family able to access the kind of entertainment choices they most enjoy, they are able to do so within a budget that suits their lifestyle.

Vaughn also alludes to another common point that was raised by some of my peers when she refers to the "cheesy" or "trash TV" predominant on many typical television networks. Referred to by some as "mindless junk," avoiding it and accessing better quality programming seems to be a key motivator in moving consumers to adopt streaming technology.

Artist and entrepreneur Shelley Schroeder and her family cut the cord three years ago. Says Schroeder, "90 percent of our viewing is on tablets with 10 percent on smart TVs (LG and Roku). We stream from Netflix, Crave, YouTube, and Prime. We will also rent newer movies using Google Play so we can watch them together on the TV. The cord costs a lot more and provides a ton of junk. Streaming costs less and we are able to access specifically what we want rather than hundreds of channels we don't even watch. Also, we strongly dislike commercials. Now, the only place we see commercials is on YouTube. Our child only has access to age-restricted Netflix. As parents, we are better able to monitor and control viewing options rather than simply changing TV channels so he doesn't consume content that is not age appropriate." In Schroeder's example the family has thought out their individual viewing needs as well as come up with a solution to ensure individuals aren't isolated by their screens by watching streamed rental movies together. They are also wisely using tools and technology to protect their son from the inappropriate content that is rife on the internet.

These are but two examples of the many ways that advances in home entertainment technology allow us to completely customize entertainment experience. While some of those surveyed responded somewhat surprisingly, in that they watched no television at all, there were many unique approaches to tailoring the experience. Hadis Kiani, owner of Yoga in Style, hasn't had a TV for more than 13 years. She uses a MacBook computer with a projector to watch documentaries and special movies. She considers most television watching a time waster. Linnette Weibe, a writer, prefers books to television and cut the cord three years ago. Book editor Eileen Espley uses a digital antenna for free channels. Allen LaRose, whom we met in Chapter 4, cut the cord almost ten years ago. Says LaRose, "I've used Roku, Apple TV, Fire TV, Chromecast, Netflix, Amazon Prime, Crave TV, and a long list of other streaming services. I only maintain two subscription services at a time. That, plus YouTube, tends to be more than enough to watch, though every so often I will cancel one and switch to something different just to get a new variety." Kim Louise Easterbrook, an author and lifestyle consultant, goes completely old school with a personal library of more than 300 CDs she plays on a traditional television set.

As you can see, the choices and combinations are nearly endless. The motivations for cord-cutting are varied. For some, it is simple economics, for others it about the vast amount of choice. For many, having control over what is being viewed, particularly by minors, is important, and yet others simply want higher quality shows than what is typically available on network TV.

1.1 Streaming sticks

There are many ways to watch television. Content can be streamed directly from the internet through your smart TV or onto your laptop, PC, smartphone, or tablet. You can also purchase streaming boxes like those used with Apple TV, or you can buy quite inexpensive streaming sticks. A streaming stick is essentially a tiny streaming media player that allows users to play online content such as music or videos through a digital television. The adapter (or stick) itself is a dongle that plugs into your TV's HDMI port and is powered through a USB cable. Using Wi-Fi, your smartphone or computer acts as the remote control so you can access video content from providers such as Netflix, YouTube, Hulu, or almost any kind of content from your computer browser. Some come with native remotes. Google's Chromecast, Amazon Fire TV stick, and the Roku TV stick are very common.

Depending on where you live, not all of the content on the streaming stick or a from a particular service provider will be available in your geography. A streaming stick is portable so you can take it with you when you travel. For example, if you are traveling from Canada where access to some shows might be restricted, into the United States, where there is more access to a wider choice of programming, you can plug in your stick, sign into your account, and enjoy a new selection of entertainment.

2. Gaming

Technology allows millions around the world to enjoy gaming as an individual or shared activity. According to an industry report in 2015, nearly 1.5 billion people across the world take part in computer gaming. Fifty-four percent feel their hobby helps and connects them with friends, and 45 percent use gaming as a way to spend time with the family.

Individual and multiplayer games are enjoyed on consoles, PCs, laptops, tablets, and smartphones. Social media feeds, magazines, blogs, and forums offer gaming tips and there are many online and offline communities for enthusiasts to gather and share tips, insight, and industry gossip. There are very few North American homes that do not have iterations of Atari, PlayStation, or Nintendo equipment in playrooms, toy boxes, or family rooms. I did a little research, and my list of the top 10 most popular video games of 2019 is as follows:

1. *Minecraft*

2. *Fortnite*

3. *Grand Theft Auto V*

4. *Tom Clancy's Rainbow Six Siege*

5. *Super Smash Bros: Ultimate*

6. *Red Dead Redemption II*

7. *Overwatch*

8. *Rocket League*

9. *Roblox*

10. *League of Legends*

According to Africa Perianez, CEO of Yokozuna Data, in an article for *Quartz*, the future of gaming lies in real-time personalization. Perianez says, "We are about to witness the emergence of a new generation of video games that cater to individual users. The content of these games will be automatically generated and customized to fit each player's personality and individual playstyle: Someone who likes a challenge will find it more difficult to advance to the next stage, whereas a player who prefers easy levels and rewards will find the game automatically adapted in that direction. Highly sophisticated games —such as role-playing games — will allow players to express nuanced emotions through their in-game actions." ("The next generation of video games will use AI to personalize your experience," Qz.com, accessed December 2019.)

Sean Crocker is a young gaming enthusiast. His current favorite video games include *Minecraft*, *Roblox*, and *Papers, Please*. Recently, he's added Oculus Rift virtual reality goggles to his gaming and online experiences. He was curious about what the goggles could add to his leisure time experiences. "With Oculus you can check your Facebook feed using the joystick, and it is as though you are flying. I really enjoy wearing them to watch Netflix. I can be sitting in a cabin in the Swiss Alps, eating popcorn and watching a movie." Within the gaming environment, Crocker enjoys being able to talk to other players who may also have goggles, especially in games where there is typically no verbal engagement. The best part of using the goggles, said Crocker, is that "They are an escape from reality. Not that I have a problem with reality, but it is very interesting to go into virtual reality. Your mind thinks you are in a cabin in Switzerland watching a movie on a massive TV screen, when really you are sitting on the couch at home." Crocker cautions people to be safe when using the goggles, however. "It's easy to forget when you are wearing them that you can't actually see when you stand up."

3. Micro-choice: The Personalization of Entertainment

Whether for gaming, movies, news broadcasts, or managing our entertainment choices, screens of all kinds have become a primary source of recreation and leisure time activity, especially in our homes. We are able to personalize and customize our viewing choices in almost endless combinations. Much of this is done for us as a result of data collection and machine learning.

A typical family night at home might have mom reading on her Kindle, big brother watching a Netflix movie through his VR goggles, big sister watching the evening news on a big screen TV, and little sister crafting a new music list on Spotify on her smartphone.

In terms of family entertainment, you are only limited by your budget or the robustness of your network.

7
Time to Chill:
Travel and Leisure

How do you spend your leisure time? The way you answer that question probably depends on your "age and stage." If you are nearing retirement, you may be compiling a bucket list of activities and experiences that you want to make sure to do while you are still fit and active and have the budget to do so. You may find yourself with more time on your hands as you transition to working less, looking for ways to connect socially with people who have shared interests. Perhaps you are pursuing interests you put aside in your working years such as painting, writing, crafting, or other creative pursuits. Maybe it is time to finally hone your golf or tennis game, or join a service club.

If you are fully retired, you may find yourself with more time to travel. If you are elderly, you may find travel and active physical pursuits more difficult but are still looking for ways to continue to experience the world around you, and to connect socially with family and friends. Time is precious at any age, and if you are still in your working years, or raising a family, you pursue your leisure activities in between daily work or domestic obligations. Perhaps you love to read or are an avid Netflix binger?

In Chapter 6 we talked in some detail about how dramatically music and video streaming and gaming have changed the way we access and use in-home entertainment options. In the same way that "whole home Wi-Fi" and smart technology have transformed the way we consume entertainment, manage our homes, monitor health, and transact commerce, the IoT is impacting our leisure time — from travel and tourism to leisure sports, there's an app for that.

1. Smart Travel

While working on this book I had the opportunity to take a seaplane flight from the island where I live to downtown Vancouver, BC. Generally, the flights I take of this nature are between the small coastal hubs that dot Canada's west coast. It had been some years since I had flown in or out of urban Vancouver's busy Coal Harbour.

What used to be a booking office in a small industrial trailer located in the rear of an underground parking lot has grown into a bustling oceanfront terminal boasting multiple airline services, a large and bright waiting room, gift shop, and small café. The bright, modern terminal also has its own robot, Pepper, that greets visitors and provides information about tours, baggage allowances, and booking instructions. A friendly robot, Pepper also strikes a pose, dances, and takes selfies with you. Beyond the fun and interactivity offered by onsite robots, they gather data on our traveling habits, tourist needs, and comfort level with machine interaction. Pepper is helping Harbour Air, already the world's largest seaplane company, do customer research.

The Hilton hotel chain is also utilizing artificial intelligence (AI) for face-to-face customer service with its robot, Connie. This robot uses AI and speech recognition to answer questions and provide information to customers. Human interactions help the robot learn and improve future communication. The companies learn more about what customers want and need.

Nearly every hotel, airline, transportation system, or tourist-oriented business includes smart technology to improve customer service and experience. Chatbots and online customer service technologies enable service providers to offer faster and faster response times to demanding customers. The data collected as we interface with these technologies is used to improve service and customize experiences.

For some, especially older travelers, the changes in the industry are not necessarily welcome ones. Travel transactions are moving toward the frictionless mode, much like the advances in retail shopping, and are becoming independent of human interactions. Self check-in and check-out services have become the norm. For those who are not adapted to technology this can be frustrating, but for busy, mainstream travelers, automated and smart services help people save time and money.

1.1 Travel and augmented reality and virtual reality

Sean Crocker, our young gaming enthusiast, gave us a glimpse into how he is using virtual reality to enhance his gaming and leisure time experiences at home in Chapter 6. Now, let's take a look at both augmented reality and virtual reality and how they are influencing the travel and tourism industry.

Augmented reality (AR) adds computer-generated digital elements to a real-world environment, often using the camera and GPS technologies found on a smartphone. Examples of augmented reality experiences include Snapchat or Instagram Story filters and lenses that add or enhance images seen in the screen such as adding a crown of flowers or rabbit ears to your real-time video images. A popular example of AR is the game, *Pokémon Go. Pokémon Go* uses mobile device GPS to locate, capture, battle, and train virtual creatures, called Pokémon, which appear as if they are in the player's real-world location.

Virtual reality (VR), however, is a complete immersion experience that shuts out the physical world. Using VR devices such as HTC Vive, Oculus Rift, or Google Cardboard, users can "experience" real-world and imagined environments. You can virtually swim with the dolphins, visit an Amazon rainforest, find yourself on the back of a dragon, or in a cabin in Switzerland. It is a simulated experience. Virtual reality applications are used extensively in gaming, and for medical or military training purposes. Augmented reality, and to some degree, virtual reality, is becoming increasingly popular in the travel industry.

First time travelers or those with a fear of flying for example, will find VR video a great way to get a preliminary experience of what it looks like to fly. Small planes can be especially intimidating for nervous flyers, as you are up close and personal with the experience.

While not fully immersive, taking a few minutes to watch VR videos may allay some of the fear associated with this kind of travel. These videos can also pique travelers' interest, offering a glimpse into another world. Through virtual reality, consumers can virtually visit hotel rooms, travel destinations, and even take care of booking.

> To view an example of a Virtual Reality small plane video, visit www.harbourair.com/flight-info/flight/photos-videos.

Hotels also use augmented reality to allow guests to enhance their use of travel maps, and to introduce onsite gaming aspects such as treasure hunts. Best Western hotels have used AR so that children can "see" Disney characters on their premises, and there are AR apps that allow users to redecorate rooms and place virtual celebrities in the hotel.

One of the most popular applications for AR in travel is being able to use the apps when you visit a tourist destination. Augmented reality essentially overlays images or information onto the real-world site. So, for example, you can visit an ancient ruin and see a virtual image of what it might have looked like originally. Augmented reality apps can also give you detailed information about works of art, restaurant menus, or local architecture.

Many of these innovations related to travel and tourism are possible because of our smartphones. With just a few taps, we can book flights, view and book accommodation, research destinations, call taxis, look at GPS maps, and translate text and speech as we go.

1.2 Travel apps

In an anecdotal poll of my friends and colleagues, several apps emerged as favorites for those who travel:

- Google Maps
- Expedia
- Hopper
- Booking.com
- Skyscanner

- Mobile Passport

- TripIt

- TripAdvisor

- City Mapper

There were also several specialty apps mentioned, such as the Airbnb app for accommodations, TrustedHousesitters to find house sits, and iOverlander, for finding campsites. Many mentioned the various features of Google Maps both for road trips and other travel uses. One of my colleagues, C.K. Lee, described it this way: "Google Maps saves lists of all the places I plan to visit, eat, stay — it is also easy to share with fellow travelers, both the group with you and the crew virtually following along from home. The Explore Nearby function is awesome for gas stations, sudden onsets of hunger, and other surprises." Several people also noted the convenience of downloading apps used to unlock the door of your hotel room, and particularly for utilizing Airbnb services.

Personally, I love the convenience of being able to download my favorite movies, books, or TV shows onto my iPad for travel. While nearly all airlines offer downloadable apps in order for you to access their entertainment systems, they don't always stock your favorites. You may also have to pay for in-flight Wi-Fi access, depending on the carrier. Before traveling, an excellent tip is to check for and download the apps that apply to the airline you are using, as well as the hotels where you've booked your accommodation. It is also worth researching the restaurants and tourist sites you wish to visit and downloading any apps for those as well. Safe travels!

2. Other Leisure Activities

2.1 Reading and e-reading

I find the convenience of an e-reader unparalleled. As both an avid reader and traveler, I commonly buy both a print version and an e-book version of my favorite novels, so I can have the same books available to hold in my hand and in my Kindle app on my iPad when I travel. Not only can I load dozens of books onto my tablet, I can adjust the screen brightness, font size, and page color as I read. This is really helpful, especially in low light situations, or for tired or weakening eyes. I can access my Kindle library on my tablet, laptop, PC, smartphone, and even in my car, or on my TV screen with my Amazon Fire TV stick. Delightfully, my Alexa virtual assistant can access my paid Kindle library and read aloud to me, picking up wherever I felt off in my current reading choice. I find being read to both luxurious and comforting.

There are thousands of books available as ebooks, and many are also available as audiobooks. Audiobooks are verbal recordings of books that are either recited word-for-word or in abridged versions. As the name suggests, you listen to the books rather than read them. Audiobooks are available for download through many public library systems or you can sign up for paid subscriptions or fee-based platforms through services such as Audible, Scribd, Audiobooks.com, or Kobo. Many of these services offer free trial periods so you can test them and see what you like. Very often the books are narrated by professional actors, celebrities, or the book's author. Currently, in the US you can also make storytime more magical by asking your Google Home smart speaker to read along. The device will supply sound effects and music to a selection of children's titles from the Little Golden Book series.

2.2 Leisure sports and hobbies

The Internet of Things has a lot to offer the leisure sports enthusiasts and hobbyists. In Chapter 9 we'll talk about the massive consumer adaptation to fitness trackers to support health and fitness goals. This sensor technology is being applied to many smart gadgets to help both professional and amateur athletes improve their game and maintain fitness.

There are smart boxing units that track your workout and display onscreen games to keep you motivated. Smart soccer balls contain motion detectors that gather data such as trajectory, spin, and force and report results in a real-time data transfer to your smartphone. There is a Tennibot for picking up tennis balls, and a smart tennis sensor that attaches to your racket recording shot data that is displayed on your smartphone via Bluetooth.

Garmin offers a GPS and laser-equipped range finder that allows golfers on more than 40,000 golf courses to see a green view overlay and full-color course view in 2D. This is an augmented reality applied to golf. Using lasers, it is accurate to within ten inches and also offers par and other course information. Competing with Fitbit, and the Apple Watch, the Garmin brand specializes in GPS technology for automotive, aviation, marine, outdoor, and sports activities.

Many types of smartwatches are customized for specific pursuits. You can find your Zen with a smart yoga assistant watch, or select a specific watch for running, swimming, golfing, or general fitness.

Wikipedia lists hundreds of hobbies. There are outdoor hobbies, indoor hobbies, hobbies that involve collecting, competitive hobbies, and hobbies that involve observing. From photography to fly fishing, innovative smart technology is being utilized to enrich the hobbyists experience. Technology itself is a hobby for some and there are new hobbies, such as geocaching. that are only possible because of technology.

For some, hobbies are a way to take a break from technology and devices. As I've said elsewhere in the book, it is not required that you connect everything in your life to the Internet of Things, but it is good to know the options.

> A great source for updates, reviews, and information on all kinds of gadgets is www.thegadgetflow.com.

2.3 Social media and communities of interest

I would be remiss if I did not mention social media communities and other online communities of interest as integral to our leisure and recreation pursuits. In my 2016 book, *#Untrending: A Field Guide to Social Media That Matters* (First Choice Books, 2016), I talked about connecting those with shared interests via social networks. I wrote, "If nothing else, the Internet has proven that there is a tribe for everyone. From cat fanciers to chicken farmers to Pyrex collectors you can find your people and spill out your giddy fascinations." No matter what your hobby or area of interest, you can be certain that you will find a community online where members are all equally fascinated by that specific subject. With our smart, connected homes, we can use our devices to connect immediately and in real time with these communities. Through video-calling apps such as Skype, Zoom, and FaceTime, we can be in real time conversations at the tap of a screen or via voice command. Virtual reality technology allows us to be together in virtual physical form, at least via our avatars.

8
Smart Shopping

As we've examined smart technology not only for use in our connected homes, but also how it applies to our leisure and free time activities, we've seen how automation and personalization has changed our expectations as consumers. We've come to expect a very high degree of responsiveness from businesses and services. Communication is immediate, and in real time, and crosses the boundaries of geography and space. Machine learning and artificial intelligence is being applied in every area of our lives enabling highly sophisticated data-driven marketing and advertising. This has radically changed the way we live, work, play, and make transactions. Retailers have been quick to adapt, and certainly the influence of the online shopping giant Amazon, has fundamentally changed the way we shop.

From changes to the in-person shopping experience such as automated check-out, beacon apps that trigger preset actions delivering personalized experiences to your phone while you stand in the store, to robots roaming the aisles at Target, brick and mortar stores are now "smart" too.

Accessing products and services online has become common shopping practice. To the frustration of some, many products and services can now only be accessed online. Service appointments for everything from oil changes to pedicures can be booked via scheduling apps. My dentist texts me reminders for hygiene appointments and an automated robocall confirms medical test times including detailed preparation instructions. I receive similar reminders from my favorite retailers, and the websites I have visited when I am browsing for products and services.

Let's take a look at how smart technology has redefined our shopping habits.

1. Shopping Online

Recent statistics show that somewhere around 96 percent of visitors to a website leave without buying. How do we know? As discussed in Chapter 3, data is being collected nearly every time we tap, type, or voice search. Savvy businesses and organizations want to know as much as possible about their customers and clients, whether this is to improve services or to sell more products. Websites make use of tools such as "cookies" — small text files — to track when you first visit a site, when you return, and your site preferences. This is how sites remember what's in your shopping cart and get to know your browsing habits. By gathering and analyzing the data, advertising can be very specifically targeted, or retargeted, based on your interests.

Retargeting is the way brands and marketers remind shoppers of their initial interest and brings them back to complete a purchase. Basic retargeting simply shows you ads for products that you most recently viewed, while advanced retargeting is more sophisticated, connecting across devices and platforms using identity matching and relying on machine learning to personalize ads with dynamic and creative optimization that will most resonate with an individual shopper.

Think of your own online browsing habits. Recently, I was on my laptop browsing for barbecue covers, looking for a customized cover for our relatively small unit. I found what I was looking for and saw that the product was in stock at my local store. The hardware store's website tracked my visit and later, while I was visiting Instagram on my smartphone, an ad for barbecue covers appeared in my feed. While this can feel like an invasion of privacy or may seem spookily prescient on the part of the internet, it is an excellent example of how machine learning and sophisticated technology captures our data, analyzes our interests and behavior, and customizes product offerings. This kind of machine learning is the basis for the IoT.

I use this not only as an example of smart technology as applied to online shopping, but also to illustrate the myriad choices available to consumers to customize their shopping experience. I searched online for "BBQ covers."Google delivered me to the page of a large hardware retailer, specifically my local outlet, because GPS identified the location of my laptop. Once on the web page, I was offered the choice of changing locations. By simply entering my postal code, or using a Google map option, I was provided with a list of the nearest outlets, or should I prefer a different company, other hardware retailers near me. Satisfied with the retailer, I browsed the products until I found the item I wanted. The site noted that the particular cover I wanted was in stock. I was offered the choice of buying it online for pickup in the store, or purchasing it and having it delivered to my home for a fee. For items ordered for in-store pick up, the process is relatively simple and is one duplicated by retail outlets across North America.

Had the item not been in stock, it could have been ordered online and shipped to the store of my choice — a service that applies to thousands of items that can be shipped free of charge to a local store when you order online. Of course, I could also have ordered the barbecue cover and had it delivered to my door for a fee. In this case, the delivery fee was higher than the cost of the item, so not really a viable option. However, if I had mobility issues, was ill, or very elderly — such a choice could very well be worth it. All of the above took about five minutes. I did it on my laptop, but the same process can be done on any smartphone or tablet. As an Amazon customer, I could also have easily ordered the cover online, using the one-click feature, or using my Amazon Echo Dot smart speaker, I could also have simply had Alexa order it for me or add it to my shopping list.

Since I had a list of errands to run anyway and, thanks to the website, I knew the item was in stock locally, I added a stop at the hardware store to my to-do list and bought the item in person. Interestingly, there was quite a lineup of folks at the checkout. With only one item to scan, I chose to use the automated self-checkout.

2. Bricks and Mortar

The Internet of Things is rapidly changing the retail shopping environment. In late 2019, my husband and I relocated to a new community. Our previous community offered limited brick and mortar retail shopping opportunities. Although we had plenty of access to amenities for needed items such as groceries and hardware, we lacked local access to fashion retailers or specialty shops. I did much of my personal discretionary shopping while traveling, or as an early adapter to internet use, online.

Our new community is a central hub for smaller surrounding communities and offers a wide selection of malls, big box wholesale stores, and quaint specialty markets and shops. For me, it is a kind of shopping mecca. I am spending more time in retail stores and have noticed key changes in the in-person shopping experience. Not only are more retailers offering self-checkout kiosks as part of the experience, many are now e-commerce fulfillment hubs. As a consumer, I no longer need be disappointed, if like Cinderella's stepsisters, the available shoe does not fit, I can simply order my size in-store and have a pair delivered, either to the store for pick up, or directly to my home address.

An added benefit (or bane, depending on your point of view) is that having placed an in-store order and received the subsequent order confirmation and tracking email notifications, you will be added to a mailing list and begin receiving notifications of new products, discounts, sales, and coupons. If you prefer not to receive brand emails, in most cases you can simply unsubscribe.

Depending on where you live, anti-spam legislation may vary. In Canada and the US, all promotional emails must include an unsubscribe feature. If you are receiving unwanted solicitation emails, check the regulations in your region.

3. Cashless Transactions

Check-out free shopping? While it might feel like stealing to simply walk into a shop, pick up your products, and walk out without interacting with either a clerk or a scanning terminal, contactless payment options are on the rise. Known as frictionless commerce or frictionless checkout, it is predicted as the future of retail. WhatIs.com, part of the TechTarget network of technology specific websites (and an excellent resource of technology experts worldwide) defines frictionless payments as: "a method of using data from devices, apps and websites to integrate buying opportunities as simply and seamlessly as possible into consumers' everyday activities and natural environments."

One of the first real forays into the practical application of completely frictionless payments is the Just Walk Out technology used in the Amazon Go stores that can be found in some major metropolitan areas in the United States. Just Walk Out technology uses cameras and sensors to track what shoppers take or return to shelves as they shop. Purchases are listed in a virtual cart and shoppers are billed through their Amazon accounts. Consumers no longer need to stand in line at checkouts or navigate self-checkout kiosks.

Despite the convenience and effectiveness of the system, its rollout and adaptation has not been as robust as expected. Nevertheless, Amazon continues to pilot this and other new enhanced checkout solutions.

In 2016, Walmart introduced Scan and Go technology. Essentially, customers walk around the store with a handheld scanner, scan their items, and bag them as they place them in the cart. Consumer adaptation was slow, and Walmart scaled back Scan and Go and increased self-checkout and other more seamless options. Consumers, it seems, are not quite ready for a completely frictionless shopping transaction.

Nevertheless, retailers continue to compete to improve the customer shopping and checkout experience. In October of 2019, Sobeys, a Canadian grocery giant, began piloting smart shopping carts in a suburban grocery store in Oakville, Ontario. The carts feature multiple cameras, a scanner, scale, and payment system. Just above the push bar, a touchscreen displays purchased items and in-store specials and promotions. Future software updates are planned to add multiple cameras to eliminate the need for the customers to scan items. Using machine learning and artificial intelligence, the carts can become interactive, helping grocery shoppers locate items in-store or recommending complementary products or recipe ingredients. Early feedback from customers is positive, but only time will tell if this is the shopping cart of the future. ("Sobeys unveils Canada's 1st smart grocery cart, promising a 'frictionless' shopping experience," CBC.ca, accessed December 2019.)

At the time of this writing, the following are the three most common forms of frictionless commerce:

1. **Mobile applications:** Used most notably by ride-sharing companies (think Uber or Lyft — see Chapter 10) and the Amazon

Just Walk Out technology. These apps sync with your credit card, bank account, or customer account and process payments automatically.

2. **Mobile wallets:** A digital wallet, or e-wallet allows you to make electronic transactions either with a computer online or using your smartphone at a store. Money can either be deposited into the digital wallet or the wallet can be linked directly to your back account. Other personal identification, such as a driver's license or health card, loyalty cards or other credentials can also be stored. The information is passed wirelessly to the merchant's terminal, allowing you to make purchases without the physical card present.

3. **Contactless cards:** Allow you to tap, or to wave your credit or debit card near a payment terminal to pay without swiping or using a chip card reader. A benefit to both consumers and merchants, contactless cards process payments quickly and seamlessly.

Paysafe, a leader in the online payment industry, tracks payment trends in the United Kingdom, United States, Canada, Germany, and Austria from both consumer and merchant points of view. Paysafe's Lost in Transaction: Payment Trends 2018 report examined the ongoing popularity of cash, the merging of cash with new digital payment formats, and the rise of contactless and digital wallets.

According to Paysafe, 40 percent of North American retailers plan to introduce checkout-free shopping within the next two years, while 36 percent of North American small- and medium-sized businesses currently accept contactless payments with 9 percent offering self-checkout options, 8 percent have order-ahead apps, and 1 percent have biometric capabilities, for example, fingerprint, facial, or voice recognition (Paysafe.com "Lost in Transaction" survey 2018.)

It's safe to say cash isn't going anywhere. While individual vendors of goods and services may try to restrict sales to debit and credit only, consumers are determined to keep using cash. In May of 2019, San Francisco banned cashless businesses, as the practice was widely viewed as discriminatory against those with low incomes who may be unable to obtain credit. San Francisco's ruling followed similar rulings in cities such as Philadelphia and New Jersey.

Adaptation to contactless or frictionless transactions may vary based on income level, or age (70 percent of millennials say they would move away from cash entirely in favor of other forms of payments) and it also varies by country, according to Paysafe, with the United Kingdom leading the world in contactless shopping. Globally, cash is still widely used, followed by credit and debit cards. For consumers, the world of shopping is changing — both online and off. Savvy retailers are committed to making sure customer service remains at the forefront while responding to emerging technologies and consumer preferences.

4. Delivered to Your Doorstep

Most of us are pretty familiar with home delivery services. While personal, or "snail mail" is on the decline, we are used to having post delivered, either to our mailboxes or doorsteps. As a youngster, one of my great joys was the arrival of the Christmas catalog. Major department store retailers, at least in Canada, issued a thick, glossy printed color catalog that arrived at our house in late summer. Called the *Sears Wish Book* (aptly named) my siblings and I would pore over it, dog-earing pages and snipping out pictures of longed-for toys and clothes. Today's equivalent would be web browsing, bookmarking pages and sites, the Amazon Wish List, and sending links back and forth via email or text message to parents, grandparents, and generous aunts and uncles to add to gift wish lists.

As a bit of a lark, I asked my Alexa smart speaker what I should get my husband for Christmas. Alexa offered the following poetic response:

How about drum cymbals, gold thimbles or a holiday sweater, some climbing rope, a telescope, or a big jar of hot peppers?

For that Trekkie, something techy, like a gadget for spaghetti.

There's always wool socks, a wood box, or a ball that can bounce.

No matter the gift that you give, it's the thought that counts.

I laughed out loud at this response. Not only was it entertaining, some of the suggestions are actually not bad. Despite feeling fairly sure wool socks, a gadget for spaghetti, and a telescope would be good bets, I asked Alexa for recommendations for books on urban planning. Alexa wasn't able to process this request, however Google Home handily offered up an excellent suggestion. As we discovered in Chapter 4, not all voice assistants are equal in their ability to respond. I ordered Google's suggestion online (rather ironically on Amazon) and the gift was delivered within a day or two to my door.

A friend of my mother's recently moved into a new, smart condominium complex. The building features many innovative features, but its designers clearly anticipated the rise of online shopping and its integration with home delivery. Each tenant is provided with a relatively spacious and attractive storage locker in the lobby of the building. An individualized electronic access code is also provided. Tenants can provide this code to delivery people whether they are delivering takeout, groceries, or online shopping purchases. Access to the building by delivery people is restricted to the lobby and each storage locker is secure. This is a great example of the integration of smart buildings with smart shopping, and advanced planning on the part of the site developer.

It is important to understand these trends and to consider how they impact your personal choices around shopping preferences and the technology that supports a positive experience for you and your family. If you are comfortable with cash, other than a few specialty retailer exceptions, it is still a viable currency. Tapping, swiping, and inserting credit and debit cards will continue to be common transactions.

In researching shopping options for this book, I did not find much in the way of mainstream studies that examined the role of Bitcoin and other cryptocurrencies in the current retail shopping environment. Cryptocurrency is a digital currency that is decentralized and controlled by its users and computer algorithms, called blockchain, to maintain its integrity. The currency is still relatively new, with most of the interest in it in the last decade coming from investors rather than consumers. However, according to a May 13, 2019 Fortune.com article, "Bitcoin Comes to Whole Foods, Major Retailers in Coup for Digital Currency," several major retailers including Crate and Barrel, Nordstroms, and Whole Foods are poised to begin accepting cryptocurrency.

You can expect a rise in self-checkout kiosks and more testing of frictionless transactions such as Just Walk Out and advanced versions of Scan and Go, such as smart shopping carts. Despite the early lack of consumer uptake, retailers will continue to experiment with innovative technology. Retailers have unprecedented access to consumer purchasing data and the enabling technology to incorporate machine learning, artificial intelligence technology, augmented reality, and personalized advertising tailored to the individual consumer experience.

9
Smart Health and Fitness

Most of us are familiar with Twitter, Facebook, Instagram, and Snapchat. These are apps that help us connect with friends and loved ones and share the details of our day-to-day lives and support social interaction. What about apps that support health and wellness? There are literally thousands of apps available in the consumer marketplace to support personal fitness, health, stress-reduction, and diet goals. Public interest is growing in these apps and the devices that support them, and medical and health professionals are at the forefront of developing and integrating emerging digital health technologies with patient care.

We can access Dr. Google to research and investigate everything from cures for the common cold to the implications of more serious and complex medical diagnoses (though consulting an actual doctor is always a better idea than trying to sift through the information and self-diagnose). As patients, throughout most of North America, we have direct access to our personal health records and lab test results and can arrive at consults with doctors and specialists armed with detailed background information and relevant questions. We are more empowered than ever to understand and make important health-care choices. But can we understand what is happening inside our bodies

— how we react to medications, how our individual systems respond to diseases?

Thanks to digital technology, that day is dawning. There are smart pills that can be tracked once swallowed, ("'Smart' pills are here and we need to consider the risks," CNN.com, March 17, 2019), and smart pill boxes to help people remember when to take important medications. Data collected through apps and sensor technologies can be analyzed and used to devise tailored-to-you individualized treatment and therapy. The same technologies that drive and support the IoT in our smart cars and smarthomes are being used to support smart health.

Sensor technologies can be integrated into watches, armbands, adhesive bandages, or clothing and collect data on everything from cardiac rhythm, heart rate, blood pressure, respiration, oxygen saturation, galvanic skin response, glucose levels, body temperature, body motions, and ambient temperature, to global positioning. This means that patients with chronic diseases can be monitored remotely, in real time, no matter where they live. Through the use of teleconferencing, timely, patient-centered care can be coordinated virtually amongst multiple providers.

1. The State of Digital Medicine

In 2019, I had the opportunity to share the stage with Dr. Kendall Ho. Dr. Ho was the keynote speaker for an innovation forum hosted by the city government in my local community. Dr. Ho is an emergency medical specialist at the Vancouver General Hospital, and a professor in the University of British Columbia Faculty of Medicine Department of Emergency Medicine. He leads the Digital Emergency Medicine Unit, and conducts research on sensors and wearables, health apps, data analytics, and virtual health. Dr. Ho works with researchers worldwide and has received both provincial and national awards for his work. Much of his research centers around the health applications of sensor technologies. An important aspect of his work in the field is the education and training of health professionals, patients, and the public on how to optimize the use of technologies for health. Dr. Ho calls this "digital health literacy."

At the time of writing this book, Dr. Ho is leading a study to determine how digital technologies supports patients between hospital and home. The study, TEC4Home (Telehealth for Emergency-Community

Continuity of Care Connectivity via Home Tele-monitoring), is an initiative of the University of British Columbia and Vancouver Coastal Health. I had the opportunity to interview Dr. Ho and we discussed the way technology is transforming patient care.

"I was always interested in how we can help patients to safely transition from the hospital to the home and how we can monitor them once they are home," said Dr. Ho. "Our results indicate that home use of wearables and sensors for patients with, for example, heart failure or living with COPD (Chronic Obstructive Pulmonary Disease) can reduce hospital readmissions by half within 90 days.

"Within one to two years patients will have access to much more than just lab tests. It is a very exciting time, and the question is: How do we prepare to go there? We are at the ground level of digital health. The future of digital health has to be co-creative between the general public and health professionals. If we are to be successful at designing technologies that people will use, this dialogue is critical."

In part, it is consumers who are driving this revolution in health care. Wearables such as Fitbit, Garmin, or Apple Watches help us track diet, exercise, sports performance, sleep patterns, and the number of steps taken each day. Consumers and sport and fitness enthusiasts quickly adapted to these technologies when they were new. Health professionals anticipate that we will also adapt to more formal versions of monitoring and tracking and integrate these with our personal health-care plans.

2. The Doctor Is Virtually In

Telemedicine, anyone? Depending on where you live you may have a hard time accessing medical services. Where I live in Canada, it is very difficult to get a GP (a general practitioner physician who does not specialize in one particular area of medicine). Typically, the GP is the family doctor providing routine health care such as physical examinations and immunizations. They assess and treat many different conditions, including illnesses and injuries. If your doctor retires, or you relocate, it can be next to impossible to find a new family doctor in a timely way. While we have excellent hospitals and emergency services where I live, there are too few doctors to serve the needs of the regional population. For others, who may live in very remote areas or who have mobility issues, accessing a hospital or clinic may not be physically or geographically possible. The kinds of digital health solutions discussed above will be a real boon to patients without access to facilities. Via technology, patients can self-monitor and minute-by-minute health data can be uploaded to their physician or medical services team and consultations can take place via telephone or video-chat. As well, there is a plethora of new apps, designed primarily for nonemergency medical concerns, that enable individuals to access a wide array of medical services.

Telemedicine, according to TechTarget's HealthIT, is "the remote delivery of healthcare services, such as health assessments or consultations, over the telecommunications infrastructure. It allows healthcare providers to evaluate, diagnose and treat patients using common technology, such as video conferencing and smartphones, without the need for an in-person visit." Primarily this form of remote service is delivered via apps that are easily installed on smartphones, tablets, or computers. App-delivered services can include telehealth, telecounseling, and telepsychiatry. This includes urgent care if you are sick, chronic care to help you manage ongoing health conditions, preventative care to help patients make healthy day-to-day choices, and behavioral health treatments.

A key advantage of telemedicine is convenience. Appointments can be made in real-time, and on short notice and do not require travel time or have associated costs that might be related to taking time off work, or paying for transit, gas, or childcare. This gives patients increased access and control. Because the system is based on patient convenience, it can reduce cancellations and no-shows for service providers.

Security and privacy are concerns, however. As with any technology, telemedicine systems can be vulnerable to hackers and data breaches. As well, there are restrictions on services such as prescribing medications, and these vary from jurisdiction to jurisdiction. Not all services will be available everywhere. The apps listed in section 2.1 are located in the United States, Canada, and the United Kingdom. This is by no means a definitive list of telehealth providers. A quick Google search confirmed that similar services are available in other countries as well. New Zealand, for example, has an online telehealth resource center that acts as a forum offering guidance and resources for people who want to set up, improve, or use a telehealth service within New Zealand.

2.1 Telemedicine apps

Healthline.com, ranked by *USA Today* as a top health information website, lists the following as the top telemedicine apps of 2019:

- MDLive (US)

- Lemonaid (US)

- LiveHealth (US)

- Express Care Virtual (US)

- PlushCare (US)

- Doctor on Demand (US)

- Amwell (US)

- Babylon (UK and Canada)

- Talkspace

- Maple (Canada)

Most telemedicine apps include the following services:

- Automated prescreening

- Practitioner selection and appointment scheduling

- Consultation and treatment via secure video or phone chat

- Access to patient health records

- Online documentation of consultation

- Sending prescriptions electronically

Users download their preferred app and sign up for services. Signup is relatively simple. You will need to provide personal information such as your first and last name, email address, and home address. You will need to create a password for your account. (As noted in Chapter 3, be sure to create a secure and unique password.) You will be asked to agree to the terms and conditions of use and you will be able to read the policy details that outline how the service provider collects, uses, discloses, and otherwise processes and protects your personal and medical data. You will also be asked to provide your health card identification number, or other medical insurance ID.

I recently signed up for Babylon by TELUS Health, and in order to test drive it, booked an appointment with an online doctor to have a prescription refilled — a fairly common request, I assume. Following a set of screening questions asked by a chatbot, including identifying my gender and age (there is a requirement to be 16 years or older to use the service), I opted to book an appointment. At this point further identification was required, including photos of my driver's license, and a selfie photo to compare with the photo ID. I was further given the option of having my consultation record forwarded to my family doctor by inputting her name and contact information. A map search function was available to locate my GP's office geographically. I opted to have a recording of the consultation e-filed with my personal health records. Less than 30 minutes later, I was consulting with an MD, and a temporary prescription was written. The doctor's consultation notes were recorded in the app, as well as details of my prescription. I was sent a confirmation notification and once I tapped and confirmed the prescription it was sent to the pharmacy of my choice. I picked it up the next day. (As a side note, I chose to review my experience with the app and received a rather nice note of thanks via email from their support desk.)

All in all, my experience was a positive, user-friendly one. In most cases, downloading the health app is free, but depending on your national health coverage or individual medical insurance plan, online services may involve membership fees or fees for consultations. Without an insurance plan, the typical fee per visit seems to average between $50 to $100 USD. This, of course, varies from service to service. Fees can be paid online via credit card. Medical insurance and extended health plans vary from country-to-country, and within regions. Check with your health-care insurance provider to find out what services are covered.

3. Staying Healthy: An Overview of Health and Fitness Apps

As we discussed in the first half of this chapter, much of the momentum driving digital medicine has come from the convergence of technology and consumer adaptation. Certainly in North America there is broad public interest in personal health and fitness. There are multitudes of diet and exercise programs available, and while fads come and go (does anyone else remember the Atkins diet, originally promoted by the physician Dr. Robert C. Atkins in 1972?) our interest in sustaining a healthy lifestyle persists. Consumers have been quick to adapt to using Fitbits, Garmins, and Apple Watches to track and analyze fitness habits.

3.1 Fitness trackers

A fitness tracker is a small wearable device that tracks aspects of personal wellness such as physical activity, exercise, food, weight, and sleep. Some simply count steps taken in a day; others monitor heart rate, sleep, or caloric intake, and some integrate a number of features. They vary greatly in their design and functionality but most include a display screen for quick updates, notifications when you have achieved a goal or when you need to get up and move, and the ability to pair with a smartphone app that allows you to sync your performance data. On their own, fitness trackers offer no guarantee as a way to improve fitness but they do provide a way to monitor your overall performance and stay motivated. In general, they include the following features:

- Track real-time day and night activity in regard to exercise, food, weight, and sleep.

- Sync personal stats from your device to your smartphone or computer.

- Set goals and track progress through online or mobile tools that display results on a digital dashboard.

Many trackers, such as Fitbit, widely acknowledged as a brand leader in the fitness tracking industry, include social features as well, allowing you to connect through the app with friends, family, or other Fitbit users to cheer each other on or engage in group challenges. Recently, Fitbit released a new product that integrates Alexa into the device.

My sister, Etanda Morelli, is an active, vital, middle-aged mother of two who runs a business and enjoys travel, water sports, and golf. She relies on her Apple smartwatch to provide information and motivation to support her active lifestyle. While she uses a Bushnell's smart rangefinder on her golf bag to hone her golf swing, on a daily basis she uses the Apple Watch on her wrist to meet her fitness goals.

Even though she has a very healthy lifestyle, Etanda was diagnosed with high blood pressure in her mid-20s, likely caused by genetic factors. Her smartwatch not only helps her stay on track in terms of meeting her goals for activities such as outdoor walking, it also monitors her heart rate, and acts as a reminder to stop, relax, and breathe. She hasn't yet integrated it with a blood pressure monitor, although that will likely be the next step. Says Etanda, "I want to track my activity on a day-to-day basis and with the smartwatch it is easy. I can set a goal for how many steps I want to take, or calories I want to burn. It is excellent for accountability and motivation. If I check the watch and if I see that I am very close to achieving my daily goals, I get that extra bit of motivation to continue." For Etanda, keeping her activity level up and her blood pressure down is an important life goal. She plans to stay healthy and fit and smart technology is helping her do that.

3.2 Mindfulness apps

It has become widely accepted that meditation and mindfulness practices contribute to health and well-being. Benefits include a reduction in stress levels, anxiety, depression, and insomnia, and their associated physical effects. These practices are also useful for understanding the habits and patterns of the mind and cultivating new, more focused states of being. In our fast-paced world, the quest for calmness is a growing one and the technology sector and app developers have been quick to respond with a plethora of mindfulness and meditation apps.

Apps are available with both free and paid platforms. Basic free features usually include a time-limited free trial or mini-lessons accompanied by your choice of a soothing soundscape such as rain falling, a crackling fire, or a gentle stream. Accompanying images are often nature-based. Users can select the kinds of issues they are concerned with such as stress, anxiety, sleeplessness, and so on and select corresponding meditation or mindfulness exercises. Subscribers have access to a much wider range of services and customization and most apps offer subscribers smart features such as personal analysis via mood check-ins and progress-trackers. Based on your profile, the app will recommend choices and you can adjust your sessions accordingly. Some offer badges and rewards for progress, others enable you to connect with other users, and many provide access to teachers and thought leaders in the mindfulness field.

Many people, including me, are trying to reduce or manage time spent on devices so there is a certain irony to using smartphone apps to decrease phone dependence and increase mindfulness. Despite this conundrum, these apps are a valuable tool to learn about meditation and mindfulness, develop a practice, track and analyze progress, and ultimately increase health and well-being.

Technology itself can be draining. The steep learning curve required, the constantly changing and ever-burgeoning array of choices can be overwhelming. It is common to experience "tech fatigue," particularly as you set up, maintain, and adapt to the world of the IoT. It's okay to take a rest from technology. We are humans and we move at a human pace. As consumers, we are free to choose what to embrace as part of the latest tech revolution.

You need not add Alexa or Google Home to your household, nor are you required to trade in your dumb toaster for a smart one. Give yourself permission to step away from the online environment and its associated gadgets and nurture the human relationships that nourish you. The answer to fatigue is rest. Despite the irony, if it helps, let's consider using the apps themselves to give us some respite.

The CNet.com article "11 meditation apps for better sleep and less stress" (accessed December 2019), offers the following list as recommended apps for less stress and better sleep. "In addition to ratings and favorable reviews, I looked for apps that offer more than just audio meditation. Throughout this list, you'll find options for customizable meditations, background music without words, engaging activities, inspirational push notifications and supplemental meditation or relaxation podcasts."

- Stop, Breathe & Think
- Calm
- Buddhify
- Insight Timer
- Omvana
- Simply Being
- MindWell
- Headspace

- Simple Habit

- Ten Percent Happier

- The Breathing App

Use Worksheet 5 to determine your own digital health literacy and whether or not smart technology can support your health goals.

Worksheet 5
Your Digital Health Literacy

1. **Internet Use**

   A growing number of people are using the internet to learn about health issues, lifestyle choices, and self-care strategies. What about you? Caution is required here because of the large amount of health misinformation on the internet.

   a) How often do you use the internet to learn about physical symptoms, treatments, and self-care strategies?

   ☒ Frequently   ☐ Sometimes   ☐ Rarely   ☐ Never

   b) How often do you use the internet to learn about mental health issues and well-being?

   ☐ Frequently   ☒ Sometimes   ☐ Rarely   ☐ Never

   c) Do you trust the health information you're getting online?

   ☒ Yes   ☐ No

   d) Have you made an effort to identify one or more trustworthy health websites that are clearly based on medical science?

   ☐ Yes   ☒ No

   e) Do you have a process for looking up medical definitions if you run into a term you don't understand?

   ☐ Yes   ☐ No

   f) Would you consider using the internet to compare the information you get from a good online source with the advice you're getting from your doctor?

   ☒ Yes   ☐ No

   g) Do you think you have the digital skills you need to navigate the internet for reliable health information?

   ☒ Yes   ☐ No

   h) Do you think it would be helpful to take an online course or an in-person course to improve your digital skills so you could learn more about health topics?

   ☒ Yes   ☐ No

2. **Health Records**

   In the region, state or province where you live, you may have online access to your own medical records. This could help you to better understand your health symptoms and your doctor's advice.

   a) Do you know if you can get access to your health records where you live?

   ☒ Yes   ☐ No

   b) Have you asked your doctor if you can get access to your health records?

   ☒ Yes   ☐ No

Worksheet 5 – Continued

c) Do you feel confident that you would have a good level of understanding of your health records?

☐ Yes　☒ No

3. Health and Technology

Technology offers a growing number of online tools (for example apps on smartphones) and wearables for tracking your health.

a) Do you use an online tool or a wearable to track any of the following?

	Yes	No
Daily physical activity	☒	☐
Heart rate	☐	☒
Diet	☐	☒
Blood sugar level	☐	☒
Weight	☐	☒
Blood pressure	☐	☒

b) Would you consider using a digital tool to help you manage your health?

☒ Yes　☐ No

c) If you have a family member or friend with a disability, would you recommend the use of a wearable health tool to help them avoid falls, or send a signal when they are lost or in distress?

☒ Yes　☐ No

d) Are you aware that data gathered by digital tools may be shared with third parties?

☒ Yes　☐ No

4. Telemedicine

In the world of health care, doctors and other professionals are making increasing use of patient data to prescribe or advise on treatment from remote locations.

a) Do you know if your doctor is part of a network that exchanges patient information or provides online consultation and treatment?

☐ Yes　☒ No

b) Would you feel confident about receiving treatment from a doctor or another professional through an online channel if you had never met them in person?

☒ Yes　☐ No

c) Would you feel comfortable with your consultation, test results, treatment plan, and prescription records being exchanged online between health-care professionals?

☐ Yes　☐ No　☒ Somewhat

Using digital tools and online records can help you take control of your health. You may want to have a conversation with your doctor about where to find reliable information on the internet, how to access your personal health records, and the use of online tools to track your health. You may also find that some of your friends and family are using some of these tools to improve their health.

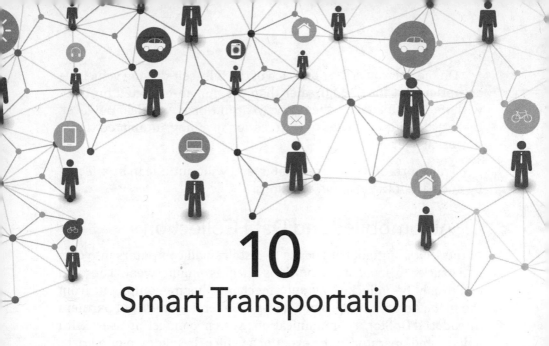

10
Smart Transportation

It has only been 100 years since the personal automobile became a common consumer item in North America, and less than that in other parts of the world. The affordable ownership of automobiles has enhanced our freedom to move and revolutionized the way we build our cities. In the United States and Canada, the personal vehicle is by far the most popular choice for commuting, shopping, and recreational travel.

The trend in automobile ownership has been toward more and more choice — an ever-wider selection of brands, vehicle types, and fuel options. The arrival of smart technology brings new levels of choice, both for vehicle owners and for those who would rather avoid the drawbacks of ownership.

If you are considering the purchase of a new vehicle in the near future, there are options in today's marketplace that were not available ten years ago. Choosing a vehicle with advanced automatic technologies may be the safer way to go, and it may reduce your insurance costs. Or you may choose to live without a private vehicle, and rely on ride sharing, ride-hailing, or public transit alternatives.

On the horizon is the approach of the fully self-driving vehicle — an option that may be far safer than the human-operated product, with its 40,000 fatal crashes every year in North America. However, there are major obstacles to the creation of a fully automated transportation fleet.

Transportation is an area that is, and will continue to be affected by and part of the Internet of Things.

1. Automobiles and Data Collection

In the 1990s, automakers began to install small computers into cars and trucks to measure conditions such as engine wear. The data could only be unlocked by auto mechanics using equipment from the manufacturer. In the same decade, General Motors and partners introduced OnStar, a communications system connecting users with a dedicated operator in the event of a vehicle breakdown or a crisis. By 2000, the operator could link you to a third party, give advice on navigation, or unlock your car doors.

In today's world, in-vehicle computers — or "carputers" — send constant streams of data directly to the manufacturer. Volumes average 25 gigabytes of data every hour, or as much as 4,000 gigabytes a day by some estimates. This direct link was introduced to the market without publicity around 2015 ("Your car is watching you. Who owns the data," RollCall.com, April 9, 2019).

Peter Holley, writing in *The Washington Post*, says the data from carputers is helping manufacturers to understand consumer driving habits as well as buying habits, such as what kind of fuel they use. Describing an auto purchase in California, Holley says the driver's new car would report to the people at Honda on "where he shops, the weather on his street, how often he wears his seat belt, what he was doing moments before a wreck — even where he likes to eat and how much he weighs." This technology has become almost unavoidable. Holley forecasts that every new vehicle sold starting in 2021 will be "connected," with the on-board software regularly updated from a central source. ("Big Brother on Wheels," *The Washington Post*, January 15, 2018.)

Much of this vehicle data is generated in visual form. Security cameras record external events, and this data is available to both the vehicle owner and the manufacturer. If your vehicle lacks a security camera feature, you can purchase it as an add-on at automotive accessory stores or electronics outlets. Tesla, a company whose sole product is electric cars, began to install internal cameras above the rearview mirror in its Model 3 in 2018. These cameras can presumably be used to generate visual data on the driver and passengers for any use, although the company says they were not activated as of 2019. Company owner Elon Musk says the eventual purpose of the cameras will be to monitor passengers on behalf of drivers who go into business. "It's there for when we start competing with Uber/Lyft," he wrote on Twitter in response to someone raising privacy concerns about the camera. "In case someone messes up your car, you can check the video." ("Elon Musk explains the camera inside Tesla's Model 3," TheVerge.com, April 19, 2019.)

All this data collection — from your vehicle, and from the other smart devices in your life — raises privacy concerns, a subject that was addressed in Chapter 3. The question of who owns vehicle data, and the privacy implications, have become a matter for discussion among lawmakers in North America and Europe. In the meantime, car makers and many other industrial interests are advertising the positive aspects of data collection. The website of the Alliance of Automobile Manufacturers presents these potential benefits:

- Automatic crash notification, bringing assistance to vehicle occupants when needed.

- Alerts about traffic conditions to reduce congestion.

- Electronic security features to help locate lost or stolen vehicles.

The US Department of Transportation's website profiles the introduction of smart vehicles as a powerful new management tool for fleet owners. "[T]he technology is becoming used more frequently in commercial operations to track trucking fleets and freight movement, monitor delivery times and driver productivity, and provide real-time updates and scheduled reporting via text or email. It is also being used to record statistics such as idle time, cruise time, hard-braking and rapid speed change events, speed, and driver hours of service."

For the insurance industry, access to vehicle data will provide an effective and indisputable way to identify good drivers and problem drivers and set rates accordingly. For families, the most common use of data-collection technology to date has been to monitor teen drivers.

However, it is worth noting that this means insurance companies are accessing data about your driving habits, via in-car trackers or companion apps installed on your smartphone. You may or may not be comfortable with this level of information about your personal whereabouts and daily activities in the hands of corporations, no matter how well-meaning.

2. Automatic Safety Features and Displays: Is Your Car Smarter Than You?

The sophistication of automotive electronics allows for the collection of vast amounts of data.

Your vehicle's computer is also used, increasingly, to protect you against collisions. Many new vehicles have front-end or rear-end sensors that will trigger automatic braking if you come too close to an object. Various alarms let you know when you have changed lanes or when another vehicle is traveling in your blind spot.

Your car, in other words, is talking to you about how to be a better driver. In some cases, it may also be telling you how to save money. While I was writing this book, my husband and I leased a Toyota Corolla hybrid; we liked the safety features, and the fact that we get more than 1,000 kilometers (600 miles) on a tank of gas. The 2020 Corolla provides us with an "eco-score" at the end of each trip, with tips on how to improve the car's fuel performance.

One caution about these automated warning and braking systems is that we may come to assume that our vehicle will always take care of us. Ryan Bradt, an instructor at the Electric Vehicle Infrastructure Training Program in Seattle, who kindly agreed to be interviewed for this book, is well-informed on the new vehicle options.

"You become very comfortable, and you begin to trust the technology," he said in an interview. "Every car I drive has a backup camera. I never look back anymore. The same with the blind spot indicator — I rarely check over my shoulder." This caution is echoed in a 2019 report on vehicle automation from the US National Academy of Sciences. It says, "many public assumptions about advanced vehicle capabilities may be misplaced. Individuals may well assume that such AVs possess much more intelligence and operational capacity than is actually the case. Such assumptions may prove critical, if not fatal."

The message is: Be careful out there. "There's always a possibility that something will fail," says Ryan Bradt. "But I think in the end, the safety benefits from these features will outweigh the concerns."

> Your smartphone is equipped with a setting that enables you to turn off phone notifications while your car is moving. As well, your phone will send a message that tells others that you are driving and can't respond. A very useful safety tip!

3. Automatic Vehicle Features and Your Insurance Policy

The cameras and sensors on your vehicle can talk to the manufacturer; they can also talk to your insurance company, if you're willing to hand over the data. The car insurance business is monitoring the safety benefits from automated warning systems, based on the sharing and analysis of data from millions of vehicles around the world, an activity they call "telematics." For example, in a 2018 report from the Insurance Institute for Highway Safety "vehicles equipped with forward collision warning systems experience 20% fewer front-to-rear collisions causing injuries, while vehicles equipped with lane departure warnings experience 21% fewer injury-causing lane departure collisions."

After we leased our Corolla, with its front and rear sensors, automatic braking, and blind spot warning system, we were rewarded with a 10 percent discount on our annual insurance premium by our Canadian insurance company. This type of discount is based on the big-picture association between automated features and fewer vehicle crashes. But the insurers want to know more: They want to find out about your performance as an individual driver.

For example, Allstate operates a "Milewise" program that ties your insurance cost directly to the distances you drive. Participants receive a thumb drive that they insert in their vehicle's computer port, and at the end of each trip they can see how much they paid in insurance.

The Progressive Casualty Insurance Company's Snapshot program is designed to reward careful drivers. Through either a mobile phone app or a thumbnail drive, Snapshot tracks hard braking, which a company spokesman says is linked to tailgating, and therefore "highly predictive variables for predicting future crashes." If you have a habit of braking suddenly, you may not get your potential insurance discount when your performance is evaluated after six months. The app emits a little beep every time you brake too hard; this is to encourage you not to tailgate. Liberty Mutual and its affiliates offer RightTrack, which helps the insurer calculate your premium based on the distances you drive, the time of day you drive, and your acceleration and braking habits. Liberty states that some drivers have reduced their annual costs by as much as $500.

"All this marks a huge change in our level of engagement with our customers," said Ginger Purgatorio, Allstate's senior vice-president for product management in an interview in November 2019. "We've always collected data; but what telematics does is allow us to rate the driver's actual performance rather than how we assume the driver is behaving."

Where I live in British Columbia, as in some other Canadian provinces, core vehicle insurance is provided through a government-run monopoly. While private insurers compete to attract low-risk drivers, the Insurance Corporation of British Columbia must provide service to everyone, in a jurisdiction that sees 300,000 vehicle crashes every year. Through 2020-2021, ICBC is piloting a telematics project focused on improving the habits of people with fewer than four years of experience behind the wheel.

Inexperienced drivers are three times as likely to crash, said Mark Milner, ICBC's manager of road safety programs, in a 2019 interview for this book. "Using a smartphone app and a windshield sensor, we're measuring speeding, hard cornering, acceleration, hard braking. It's like we're putting the volunteers through a fitness program at the gym. They'll be told how they're ranked in a group of more than a 1,000 people; they'll find out about the issues that are causing them problems, and we'll send them links to videos that will help them drive more safely. We want to learn what will motivate drivers to do better — is it lower insurance rates, some other kind of prize, or the comparison with other drivers? "

4. Digital Technologies and Public Transportation

Personal car ownership is popular because it's easy: You walk to your garage or your driveway, climb into your vehicle, and set your course. It's also expensive. As of September 2019, the American Automobile Association calculated that for someone who drives 15,000 miles (24,000 kilometers) per year, the average annual cost of owning a small sedan is $7,114, and the average cost of owning an SUV is $10,265. These numbers, which may seem high to some readers, include fuel, insurance, depreciation, and financing. They do not include parking. ("Your Driving Costs," American Automobile Association, September 12, 2019.)

For many North Americans, the cost of relying on public transit would be far lower than the cost of vehicle ownership, but this remains a minority preference. There are only a handful of US cities where more than 10 percent of the workforce commutes to work by transit. In Canada, the proportion in big cities hovers around 20 percent. One big deterrent to transit use is that transit trips typically take longer than a private vehicle trip to the same destination. The appearance of smart technologies is helping transit agencies to improve their performance. In systems that are up to date, transit control hubs monitor the minute-by-minute location of every transit vehicle, and this can be communicated to customers through the transit company app. This helps transit managers to address both driver issues and recurring obstacles along the route. Control staff can also diagnose electrical or engine issues from a distance, improving the chances for preventive maintenance rather than a breakdown on the road. Available features on new buses include the same automatic braking and alert features that are found on smaller passenger vehicles.

For the transit user, the digital age is introducing a more predictable travel experience. In many cities, we can use a transit app to find out the expected arrival time of any transit vehicle at any stop. We tap on to the bus or train with a digital pass that we reload when we have the time. The robo-voice in each transit vehicle tells us where it is going and prompts us at every stop. Changeable message signs advise us of any issues in the system, such as station construction or upcoming holiday hours. At a higher level, private-sector designers are introducing apps that will allow travelers to integrate their travel plans across several modes, with maps and schedules for public transit, airports, ferries, and taxi services. City Mapper, for example, is a free app that covers major US and Canadian cities.

The fact remains, however, that transit buses are trapped in a sea of cars, regardless of the power of their communications systems. The local bus service that stops every few blocks will continue to be slower than the trip in a private vehicle. In one scenario, this will change when the roads are handed over to driverless vehicles that can be centrally controlled. In this world, buses may get priority over single-occupant vehicles, and transit users will be rewarded. However, as discussed below, we may be waiting for this world for many years.

4.1 Car sharing

If you live in a city and you want to reduce your transportation costs, you may want to consider car sharing. This option is becoming easier all the time with the rise of sophisticated mobile apps. There are various business models for car sharing, including daily rental from among a pool of individual owners. In the most common scenario, the driver rents from an agency such as car2go, DriveNow, Zipcar, or Maven. Zipcar is the biggest operator in this group, and for a monthly subscription starting at $60 you get access to an app with the following features:

- Through the reservation system, you can find a vehicle that is parked close to you — on a street or in a parking garage — and reserve it for hours or days.

- The same app will unlock your car and can honk the car's horn if you lose track of it. The keys to the car are kept in the car at all times.

- Through the app you can reach Zipcar's customer support.

The car2go app lets customers see each car's fuel gauge or charging status during the registration to avoid unpleasant surprises. It also provides a map that guides the customer to free parking areas — either public parking or designated car2go parking spots.

Southwestern British Columbia has Modo, a cooperative with more than 800 cars, SUVs, and trucks. For a $500 (Canadian) lifetime share purchase the member receives a fob that provides access to any Modo vehicle, with rental rates of $4 per hour up to a maximum of $52 per day.

4.2 Ride hailing

The rise of the mobile app has also contributed to the creation of virtual taxi companies that will supply a driver at short notice and at a lower cost than established taxi companies. The driver could be anyone who wants to make extra cash. He or she will show up in an unbranded car — his or her own car, most likely — and is expected to maintain certain standards of vehicle maintenance and behavior if they want to keep driving. Companies such as Uber and Lyft, who are doing business in many North American cities, can provide you with an app that will —

- reserve a driver for now or later;
- let you know where your driver is, and provide you with a photo of the driver and a car plate number;
- track your progress during your ride so your friends and family always know where you are;
- choose a particular driver, if you have established a relationship; and
- report back to the company on your experience.

On the downside for the consumer, the ride-hailing driver is free to refuse your call if they don't like the look of your home neighborhood or your destination. This is a contrast with city-regulated taxi companies, which are obliged to take you where you want to go.

Uber and Lyft offer income opportunities for people who like to drive and are open to casual work. Working as an Uber driver may be something you want to consider. However, the financial returns vary wildly from city to city.

In 2019, the team at Ridestar.com conducted interviews with 2,625 Uber drivers in the United States and found that hourly revenues for drivers range from a high of $25.55 in Honolulu to a low of $4.94 in Akron, Ohio. From their hourly rate — let's say, $17.52 in Boston — they have to deduct the costs related to fuel, maintenance, commercial insurance, and tolls. The study team concluded that many drivers do not make any money at all, and this aligned with their finding that most Uber drivers stay in the game for less than a year. If Uber can't attract drivers, it can't serve its customers. ("How much does an Uber driver make?," Ridester.com, September 4, 2019.)

Ride-hailing has its hard-core supporters based on its low price, but it is not clear that this transportation option is sustainable. Uber, the largest ride-hailing company, lost money continuously during its first five years. When Uber made its first public share offering in 2019, it cautioned its investors that it may never achieve profitability. In its second quarter after the share offering, Uber lost $5 billion. Part of this may be due to research investments — more on this in section 5. — but there is also ongoing pressure on the company to improve safety and comfort levels for customers and income levels for drivers. ("Uber unveils IPO with warning it may never make a profit," Reuters, April 11, 2019.)

5. Cruising to Full Automation

The auto industry has offered cruise control as an optional feature since the 1950s. Classic cruise control has a single benefit, allowing the driver to set a cruising speed.

Active cruise control, introduced in the 2010s, senses the speed of traffic and regulates a vehicle's speed accordingly. If the car ahead slows down, you slow down. If it stops, you stop. Active cruise control represents a step towards full vehicle automation, or "driverless cars," but only a step. The International Society of Automotive Engineers has defined steps in vehicle automation; virtually all of us currently live either in Step Zero — "No Automation" — or Step One — "Vehicle is controlled by the driver, but some driver assistance features may be included in the vehicle design." ("SAE International Releases Updated Visual Chart for Its 'Levels of Driving Automation' Standard for Self-Driving Vehicles," SAE.org, December 11, 2018.)

How soon will we enter the age of the fully driverless vehicle? Trials are underway in hundreds of locations worldwide: The University of Michigan, for example, has piloted the use of a driverless automated shuttle service along a one-mile route and publicized the results. A US lobby group called the Partners for Automated Vehicle Education has grown up to advocate for increased automation: "Automated vehicles have the potential to help reduce the environmental impact of transportation, cutting fuel usage and enabling new models of vehicle ownership that reduce the need for parking spaces in communities. And automation could reduce the roughly 6 million crashes reported every year, saving billions of dollars in damage to the economy and reducing the roughly 40,000 highway deaths that occur each year [in the US]." (PaveCampaign.org, accessed December 2019.)

Industry has invested billions of dollars in the race to put driverless cars on the road. By one estimate, Waymo (a Google subsidiary), was spending $1 billion a year on this research between 2015 and 2019, and Uber invested almost $1 billion in the same period. The technical and social issues, however, appear to be surprisingly complicated.

For example, in 2019 the California government released test results from Uber showing that in 26,899 test miles for driverless cars on public roads, the human backup drivers had to seize the wheel 70,165 times, or 2.6 times per mile. The comparable figures for Mercedes-Benz were also high, at 1.46 times per mile.

One of the key problems here is that machines are likely to "think" differently than people. An automated vehicle traveling in a mixed fleet where humans are present is almost certain to make unexpected calculations. And while humans may tolerate errors on the part of other humans — we are able to live, after all, with 40,000 vehicle-related deaths per year — we are less likely to accept machine errors.

"The public's awareness is high," says Ryan Bradt, instructor at the Electric Vehicle Infrastructure Training Program in Seattle. "But the manufacturers will have to convince people that it's safe technology. Full automation could lead to a 90 percent reduction in vehicle crashes, but there's a lot of pushback from the public."

Concerns around the driverless vehicle include the heightened possibility of intrusion or vandalism. In 2018, Google subsidiary Waymo launched a series of automated vehicle tests in the public streets of Chandler, Arizona, a suburb of Phoenix. Police reported 20 incidents of local residents attacking the vehicles with rocks, and, in one case, with a gun. In these incidents, there was actually a person sitting in the vehicle, acting as a backup driver in the event of trouble.

For the foreseeable future, then, we are likely to see a continuous increase in the partial automation of vehicles, but drivers will continue to stay alert in case they need to take the wheel.

More information on Driver Assistance technologies is available at the (US) National Highway Traffic Administration: www.nhtsa.gov/equipment/driver-assistance-technologies

Use Worksheet 6 to reflect on your personal transportation needs. Are you ready for an electric vehicle or smart car?

Worksheet 6
Transportation Needs, Today and Tomorrow

Use the scale to rank your degree of comfort with the various transportation options available to you (or soon to be available), where 1 is not comfortable at all, and 5 is completely comfortable.

Mode of Transportation	1	2	3	4	5
Driverless electric car	☒	☐	☐	☐	☐
Fully electric personal smart vehicle	☐	☐	☐	☒	☐
Hybrid personal smart vehicle	☐	☐	☐	☐	☒
Public transportation (traditional bus or train)	☐	☐	☐	☒	☐
Public transportation (electric bus or train)	☐	☐	☐	☒	☐
Public transportation (unmanned or driverless)	☐	☐	☒	☐	☐
Car sharing/shuttle services	☐	☐	☒	☐	☐
Ride hailing services (Uber/Lyft)	☐	☐	☒	☐	☐
Traditional taxi service	☐	☐	☐	☐	☒
Other (List)	☐	☐	☐	☐	☐

Now answer the following questions:

1. Do you absolutely need one or more personal vehicles?

   At this time, yes.

2. Have you calculated the annual costs of owning or leasing a personal vehicle versus the costs of other transportation modes described in this chapter?

   No

3. How concerned are you about fuel costs?

   Somewhat concerned

4. Are you concerned about the environmental impacts of fossil fuels?

   Yes

5. How comfortable are you adapting to and using new technology?

   Fairly comfortable

6. Are you willing to share driving data in order to:
   - ☒ improve driving skills
   - ☒ improve safety
   - ☒ reduce insurance premiums

7. Do you foresee needing to purchase or lease a new vehicle within the next 3-5 years?

   Yes

Think about the answers to the questions above. Consider your own comfort level with the various modes of transportation available to you. Based on your reflection, you may decide that you do not need a new personal vehicle and you are ready to use public transportation or ride-sharing options. You may feel that you are not ready to make the leap into a smart car or electric vehicle and may wish to look for a more traditional vehicle to meet your transportation needs. Remember, your transportation needs, and your comfort level while driving particularly in bad weather or at night, will change as you age.

11
The Future of the Internet: We Are Shaping It

From our connected homes, to our leisure choices, to the way we shop and get from place to place, from how we communicate to how we care for our health, the Internet of Things is shaping the world we live in and our daily choices.

In conclusion, let me offer some personal observations and perhaps some additional reassurances. If you are an early adapter to technology, or as Allen LaRose in Chapter 4, someone who leans toward the leading edge of the technology curve, you may find "living the future" as John Biehler described it a thrilling adventure and one you embrace with gusto. It is equally possible that you will find it overwhelming, as do many who grew up before the advent of the internet — the digital refugees referred to by Steve Dotto. You may also have some fear of technology, artificial intelligence, and where it is all going. The privacy and security concerns around the IoT are real, and in many ways even though IoT technology is still in its infancy, it is highly complex and can be difficult to understand. The good news is, that as a consumer you are largely in control. You can choose to integrate these technologies (or not integrate them) at a pace the suits you and meets your family's needs and preferences.

There will be some cases, though, where you will not have much of a choice, at least insofar as mainstream living goes. It is nearly impossible, for example, to find a pay phone anywhere in North America at the moment, so if you wanted to, you likely couldn't use one. As I pointed out early in the book, even though you may not be a person who uses a computer, you are a person who uses things. And things are becoming smarter and more integrated with the internet all the time. Home automation isn't new, and neither is the continued evolution and application of technology in our world. It is very likely over the next few years that hybrid and electric vehicles will be the norm, and there will be fewer human-to-human transactions at airport check-ins, hotels, and retail outlets. It is already very difficult to purchase new "dumb" thermostats, HVAC systems, or white goods. In the developed western world, life without a smartphone and the apps it houses is almost impossible to consider. Our children do not know a world without the internet, social media, music and video streaming, robots, and augmented reality.

We will always have some choice when it comes to adapting to technology. In my interview with Rob Richardson he pointed out that there are really two kinds of people when it comes to consumer technology: Those who put up a wall and those who have an open mind and get curious. It is my personal belief that taking on the learning curve is more empowering. This is the world we have to live in. More important, it is the world our children and grandchildren have to live in, and it is incumbent upon us to understand, guide, and lead the way to living in it wisely and well.

Much of the early promise of the internet and microtechnology turned out to be illusory. Technology has not provided us with a worry-free life of ease. There are indeed very real issues of privacy, security, and the use of our data to manipulate and control us. We must also consider the distancing effect that digital communication can have on our relationships and the potential effects of technology addiction. Advanced technology does far more than just entertain us and make daily tasks simpler. Worldwide, it is being used to improve health care, modernize critical infrastructure, and bring remote communities together. We all have a role to play in shaping the design and use of technology and plotting the course of the future. It requires us to be actively involved; to monitor our own habits; and to use our voices, votes, and pocketbooks in deciding how technology is used, and in developing the principles, legislation, and regulations that guide its use. There is no doubt that being human in a technical world is challenging. I believe we are up for the challenge.

Please allow me to support you on your journey to understanding the Internet of Things, and what it means to be fully human in a technical world. You can find me at vickimcleod.com.

Download Kit

Please enter the URL you see in the box below into your computer web browser to access and download the kit.

www.self-counsel.com/updates/internet/20kit.htm

The download kit includes:

- Worksheets from the book
- Resources for your journey into the IoT
- — And more!